CONQUER *your* SUMMIT

How to Build a Five-Year Plan & Live Your Best Life

Aliki Samone

Download the Planning Templates for Free!

Thank you for purchasing *Conquer Your Summit*. To get the most out of this book you need to download the free templates that come with your purchase.

Visit www.ConquerYourSummit.com/resources to get your copy.

Need Help Creating Your Five-Year Plan?

Sometimes planning your life can be challenging. You are not alone! If you would like to explore more help beyond the book in implementing the content in this book inquire within the link below.

The *Conquer Your Summit* community wants you to succeed in your path towards success as quickly and passionately as you can.

If you are serious about changing your current state and leveraging a proven method to live your best life, sign up today.

Visit www.ConquerYourSummit.com/coaching.

Conquer Your Summit © Copyright 2023 alikisamonestudios LLC

For more information, email aliki@conqueryoursummit.com

ISBN: 979-8-88759-516-0 - paperback

ISBN: 979-8-88759-517-7 - ebook

Illustrations from Canva

First edition 2023

This book would not have been possible without my husband—*The Summit Method* was created *because* of our partnership.

You are my guiding light, my traveling companion, and the one who always manages to find new and inventive ways to push life's limits.

Contents

Introduction

Have you ever found yourself sitting in a daze, unsure of what to do with your day? Maybe the weekend has arrived, and you don't have any plans. The thought that you should be doing something productive naturally creeps in. As you sit there thinking about the day, weekend, or maybe even the weeks ahead, the overwhelming weight of it all begins to settle into your mind:

What should I do? What am I doing with my life? How do I get to success?

This mental spiral of anxiety about your existence can make it easy to lose sight of what you should be doing and cause you to slip into complete demotivation. Your mind is hazy, and you don't know where to start. While I hope you don't experience this often, it happens to all of us in one way or another.

Good news! This book will take the stress and overwhelming feelings out of planning for success. The content before you will help you with a straightforward approach to calming your mind, easing anxiety, and helping you chart a course for today, tomorrow, and the rest of your life.

If you ever find yourself gazing at the stars, full of dreams you have come to the right place. This guide will take you on a journey to conquer your own personal summits and reach the dreams you consider to be at the top of the mountain for success.

I constantly stare into the stars, full of dreams for my life, and have many passions, goals, and journeys that I set myself on. This energizes me but sometimes all these dreams can fill me with anxiety and cause me to constantly question myself:

Am I on the right course?

When you have so much you want out of life, it can be tough to process. I realized a long time ago that I needed a method to set a course and plan to stay in the right direction. There are plenty of self-help books with corporate-minded jargon on how to make business-minded plans and execute them, but I needed something more focused on the intricacies of personal interactions and away from topics of meeting key performance objectives in a company. This system needed to have a heart and fill the soul with a bright fiery passion. I wanted to fill my life with purpose in a flexible approach that would ebb and flow with the curves thrown from every direction. I wanted to look at the mountain of all my dreams and conquer my summits.

I worked for over 10 years to develop and refine the *Summit Method* to better my life and those around me. I use it to keep to my goals, understand how to support my partner, and make the most out of daily living. Family, friends, and colleagues have used the method to unlock their potential and take the anxiety out of life planning. This method skyrocketed me into the success I have today.

I started my career out of college as an entry-level Aerospace Engineer, spiraling through years of trying to figure out what existence was supposed to be and being unhappy with where I was going. The *Summit Method* aligned me on the right course and has recorrected me multiple times since its origination. With this method, I learned to build my life from starting my career as a timid 22-year-old engineer in a big aerospace company to becoming Vice President of Program Management at a startup at the age of 29.

With a continual focus on reaching my dreams and conquering my next summit, I left the Aerospace industry at the age of 32 and have excelled in filling my life with passion projects within writing, art, and music. A dream I had for myself in high school before deciding to go into engineering instead. In those early years, I chose to focus on building a career that would support my family even if it wasn't what I truly wanted at the time. I have no regrets because I have become the person I was meant to be. Over many years of dedication, I figured out how to create a life plan to reach my dreams.

With the newfound mental freedom away from an engineering focus, I dived into a passion for creating businesses and developed passive income through a real estate investment company I co-founded that allows me to be financially free. I went from a college student who assumed she would be working in the same industry designing spacecraft for 40 years to living the life of my dreams. None of this would have been possible without the *Summit Method*.

Why do I call it the *Summit Method*? The idea here is that you are about to embark on a journey up through the incredible mountain range of life planning and are looking to get to the top of each peak along the way. The method gives you a structured approach to summit each mountain topic and find your success.

I am also an avid outdoor adventurer and have been exploring the western United States of America mountains since elementary school. In 2020, my husband and I purchased a used Mercedes Sprinter van and renovated it for camper van living. We travel to as many of nature's wonders as we can with everything we need along with us. Over the years, 'Ana the Vana', as we call the van, has taken us to over 26 National Parks (and counting!), sheltered us in countless forestland areas, and dropped us off for incredible kayak adventures through lakes and rivers along the way.

For those of you who are hikers, mountaineers, and outdoor adventurers, you know how mystical and empowering being solely in the presence of nature is. Even those who don't get into the great outdoors can't deny the incredible beauty in photographs they have seen of the towering granite cliffs of Yosemite National Park, the majestic peaks of the world's mountain ranges, or the ever-winding flow of our global rivers.

When I set out on a hike, I prepare to have everything I need for the whole day. Generally, a mountain trek is full of surprises with stream crossings, rock scrambling, occasionally some spots of snow, and a gorgeous alpine lake to find the perfect spot for lunch. This journey can be strenuous and require mental resilience to get through the uphill climb, but the rewards along the way feed my passion for continuing, for seeing what sight lies beyond the next bend. When I reach a mountain peak, there is an overwhelming flow of joy, accomplishment, and peace. I worked hard to get to that point, and I spend time there being grateful for the stunning surroundings before me.

I need to be prepared physically and mentally to climb these mountains. I must be equipped with the necessary supplies to prevail. I have spent years becoming more skilled in hiking higher and higher peaks. These skills allow me to enjoy my passion for nature while using its lessons to ascend to great heights in my own life. What nature has taught me about mental fortitude, decision-making, patience, and time has been so powerful that I want to share the theme of ascending a mountain throughout this book so that you may reach great heights in your own life.

While you will not be learning about hiking techniques and outdoor skills, this book uses the imagery of climbing mountains to paint a picture of your journey. Regardless of your experience level in planning now, after reading this book, you will have the skills to climb to the peak of your dreams—and maybe even want to try to climb a real mountain after you are done!

This book will help guide you on your journey to figure out how to create attainable goals for yourself. With the *Summit Method*, you will:

Create a *Five-Year Plan* with ease

FIVE-YEAR PLAN   TWO-YEAR ACTION PLAN

Establish a *Two-Year Action Plan* to drive progress

Set *Quarterly Goals* that give you purpose

QUARTERLY GOALS   DAILY HABITS

Learn optimal daily *Execution Habits* for success

The life you live, and the life of your dreams may be different things now, but with this book, they can be one and the same.

Still easing into what this book is about? Nobody is perfect. We all have room to grow to become the best version of ourselves. Everyone's path is different, and everyone's reasons for making a change vary. What matters is that you are choosing to confront your goals head-on and become the master of your destiny. To get there, you must learn about the *4 Mountains of Success* designed to provide you with an evenly balanced scorecard: *Personal Growth, Financial Freedom, Career Success, and Community Impact.*

To make the journey through your *4 Mountains of Success* the best it can be, you must:

- Commit to the planning strategy.

- Have an open mind.

- Cultivate a willingness to make it through harsh emotional realizations.

- Learn techniques to turn negative feelings into positive mental attitudes.

The first thing you need to do before trekking out into the wild wilderness of your life is to explore your *why* or, in other words, what you define your life purpose to be. You must set intentions to have the best toolset for the job ahead of you and spend the required time setting up your mind. You are about to start your hike to the peak of a large mountain. *Are you ready?* Probably not, and that is entirely okay. Let's go through the steps so you can know where you are headed and be the most successful leaping into the book.

To reach the top, you must start at home and pack a well-equipped bag for the expedition. I'm not talking about a tiny tote or fanny pack here. For this voyage, you need to think of mountain peaks, more like a backpacker's bag!

Why so big? Diving into your everyday existence and all its intricacies can be very challenging. It can be fun, though, if you have a great mindset going into it. You will focus on packing 3 tools for optimal success along the way.

1. Your *why* or life purpose statement

2. A *Positive Growth Mindset*

3. *Mind-Body-Spirit exercise*

Gear Up for the Climb

In **Part One** of the book, you will learn about the tools you need to pack into your backpack before starting your hike. Specifically, it will walk you through mental strength methods to bring you success. This hike is over 14 miles with an elevation gain of 16,000 feet. That's insane! I need you to be in optimal condition to get to the top, and the best way to do that is to be mentally ready to take on any obstacle.

Base Camp

In **Part Two** of the book, you will hang out at Base Camp and learn what makes up a successful life plan around your *4 Mountains of Success: Personal Growth, Financial Freedom, Career Success, and Community Impact*. This is the foundation for understanding your current life trajectory. It is in this section that you will also learn about the *Summit Event* and how it all works.

The View of Your Mountain Range: The 4 Areas of Success

In **Part Three** of the book, you will acclimate to the altitude, repack, and enjoy the views of the *4 Mountains of Success*. Each mountain is different in its own way and these chapters will walk you through how to get your baseline. You will be able to finish your current assessment after this point before getting to more challenging peaks within life planning.

Get Ready for the Climb

While continuing your trek in **Part Four** of the book, you will hit the most rewarding part of the voyage. You can no longer rely on just yourself and your mind. You will be joined by other hikers who, together as accountability partners, will lend a hand, watch for obstacles, and give the support required to make it to the top. You will gain more planning tools such as the straightforward techniques for building a *Five-Year Plan, a Two-Year Action Plan,* and *Quarterly Goals*.

Conquer Your Summits Again and Again

In **Part Five** of the book, you will bask in the light and peace of conquering your first summit. Since a summit is defined as a mountain peak in which you have set either a specific large goal or theme of goals around, you will likely not accomplish all your summits at the same time. It will take time and effort to ascend to victory on each of your goals. Here you will learn techniques for motivation and how to execute with excellence by regularly checking in with your plans. You will set up daily habits for success and be able to conquer your summits again and again.

With these five parts of the book you will perform your life plans with ease, and with all your newfound wisdom, you will have removed the overwhelming burden of not knowing what life should be. You will know how to conquer your summits, reach your dreams, and see the next level of achievement to strive for in the distance.

I spent years spiraling over not knowing what to do with my time or if I was progressing in any positive direction. I had no compass to point my way and aimlessly walked through experiences with anxiety and fear of the future. Our time on Earth is limited and seems to be flying by faster and faster each day. Wherever you are, now is the time to stop what you are doing, pick up the map to your success, and trek into greatness. You are ready to unlock your potential and become the person you were meant to be.

One Step at a Time

The best way to approach this book and have the most promising success with the outcome is to take each part of the book one at a time. You should be prepared to feel like you are reading a manual to set up the rest of your life. At the end of each chapter, you will see the immediate next steps you need to follow before moving on. To reach optimal success, you should make sure you spend the time to do this.

While the primary goal and subject is to guide you through life planning, this book will change you in many ways. I will be teaching you multiple techniques to expand your daily world. I promise that if you come into this method with an open mind for change, you will leave with the ability to know where you should be going in life. Don't procrastinate through the book. Get through the chapters, do the work, and complete your *Summit Event* as soon as possible. *What are you waiting for?* Every day you move forward in the wrong direction, you aren't living your *best life*.

As you go through this process, I want you to also think of your friends and family. Invite them to take the journey with you and grow the community of people who have changed their lives and conquered their summits. These are your accountability partners, you will need them along the way.

Next Steps Before Moving On

1. Go to www.ConquerYourSummit.com/resources to download the free worksheet templates to guide you through your planning. The book will use examples throughout the text and for best results you should follow along with your own copy.

2. Buy yourself a notebook. You will be asked to fill out this notebook throughout your journey to work through the exercises and record your inner thoughts. You will need it right away.

3. If you would prefer to use the Conquer Your Summit companion workbook, you could also purchase that and follow along chapter by chapter.

4. Continue reading to get Part One complete today! There is no time to waste in getting started with the rest of your life.

Part One

Gear Up For the Climb

With a journey into the unknown ahead of you, you'll need to equip yourself with effective mental tools for optimized success on your climb. You will learn these tools in the following chapters and pack them in your backpack. Your goal is to gear up for the climb and get to your next stop at Base Camp.

Base Camp is where mountain climbers camp out to rest and restore before setting off for their expedition. There needs to be a period of repose to truly plan and set your intentions. But before you even get there, since you're still "out in the wilderness", so to speak, making sure you're of the right mind and that you know why you're doing this in the first place is what will keep you nourished on this tricky but exciting adventure!

Let's take the time to **Gear Up!**

Chapter 1

Your Deepest Why

We each have different purposes in life. Perhaps yours is to provide for your family, create a positive community, help others, build a business, create a legacy for future generations, or retire on a private island. Regardless of your goal, finding your *why* deep inside that keeps you charging through each day is critical. So, you must dig deep—and get specific.

Your *why* should drive you to continue when the going gets tough. It should make you get up each day and push forward fiercely into your future. Is your drive to provide for your loved ones fueled by the image of their smiling faces? Did you experience a lack of support in your past that made your life goal to be creating a safe space for others? Do you want to increase your income so you can provide for yourself and others?

Thinking about all of this can be an enormous burden to carry. We tend to hide our deep emotions away and hope they stay there! For this reason, you will be given essential tools to put in your backpack to help you deal with the emotions that might come up along your journey. We will start with finding your deepest *why*—the first mental tool you need in your backpack.

To begin to think with purpose, is to enter the ranks of those strong ones who only recognize failure as one of the pathways to attainment. – James Allen

You are sitting in your living room and just signed up for the epic mountain climb called Conquer Your Summit. You read the introduction brochure, so you know the journey will have multiple phases. Today you are starting by packing your bag for

success. You have the basics for your hiking supplies, such as food, clothing, sleeping gear, survival tools, and everything the travel brochure recommended. You suddenly realize that you initially missed a stand-alone paper with big letters saying, "Don't forget the most important tools in this list!"

Your Deepest *Why*

A Positive Growth Mindset

Mind-Body-Spirit exercise

Eager to make this experience as easy and successful as possible, you spring to investigate how to acquire these tools by asking fellow mountaineers who have made the climb before. You find it peculiar that they each say the same exact thing: "Start with a Mind Map, it will guide you."

5 Minutes Can Change Your Life

It's Mind Map time! In the introduction, I mentioned that you would need a notebook, and now is the time to start using it! If you haven't picked one up yet, grab a blank sheet of paper to start, but by the end of tomorrow, make sure you stop somewhere and pick up a notebook for the rest of your journey so you have all your Mind Maps together in one place.

If you have never heard of or done a Mind Map, don't worry, it's easy. We will use Mind Map #1 as an example to get you started and it follows these basic steps.

1. In the center of a blank piece of paper, write the "topic or question" you are going to think about.

2. Set a timer for 5 minutes.

3. Start writing down ideas about the topic as quickly as possible as they come to mind. Draw little offshoot lines from the center bubble and write the idea at the end of this line.

4. If you have an idea that springs off the first ideas, you then just draw a

line from those ideas, and so on as the Mind Map grows.

> 5. If you need more time at the end of 5 minutes, set the timer again and keep going.

NOTE! All thoughts and ideas are good ones! Do not overthink them, just let your mind flow and write everything down without hindering your thoughts.

Mind Map #1: *What am I grateful for that has happened in the last year?*

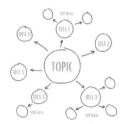

This Mind Map will be the first of many self-reflective moments for you along this journey. It will first and foremost ground you in positive energy. Focusing on the things you are grateful for is the first step in improving your state of mind.

1. In the center of your page, draw a circle.

2. Inside the circle, write your topic:

What am I grateful for that has happened in the last year?

3. Set a timer for 5 minutes and begin writing your answers to this question each in their own separate thought bubble that connects back to the middle circle with a line. There are no right or wrong thoughts or ideas. Just let it flow. Release anything and everything from your mind. Please don't limit yourself or overthink it. Nobody else will see this, so don't hold back.

4. After the 5 minutes is up, get a feel for where you are. If you need more time, set another 5 minutes and go from there. In general, you should keep Mind Mapping at 10 to 15 minutes max. This is not supposed to be perfect!

5. After your free-form Mind Mapping phase, review everything you wrote down and see if you can identify any themes in common between the different ideas.

6. Color, circle, or star items in a similar theme and start writing those main themes on a separate sheet of paper in your notebook. Make sure to do this after each Mind Map.

Mind Map #2: *What events, people, thoughts, or interactions have deeply affected you in your life?*

Now that you have the hang of it, it's time for a second Mind Map that will bring you closer to finding your deepest *why*. Get your notebook and timer ready. I want you to spend 5 minutes thinking about your life up to this point. The question for the center circle of this Mind Map will be:

What events, people, thoughts, or interactions have deeply affected you in your life?

Asking yourself this question instead of just *What's My Why?* will help you find your true *why* for wanting to improve your life, as opposed to something you think *"should"* have as your *why*. Only your true life purpose can burn bright enough to light your path along this journey.

When you hit the start button on the timer, relax and trust your intuition. Think about the good times, the difficult times, and even the times you didn't get to have but wish you could have. Explore each idea bubble you create with even more bubbles around it on why those things affected you or the emotions or consequences, good or bad, associated with that experience. By reflecting on your experiences in the past you'll find the things you care about now, which fuel you to where you want to be.

Don't forget to note any themes from your ideas in the Mind Map in your notebook.

Mind Map #3: *Are there any goals or dreams you feel you have been carrying for a lot of your life? (list reasons why they have or have not happened)*

This next Mind Map will allow you to practice listening to your inner voice. This time, in the center circle, write:

Are there any goals or dreams you feel you have been carrying for a lot of your life?

(list reasons why they have or have not happened)

As you start the timer for 5 minutes, think about your dreams, what makes you happy in life, and any passions you have carried over time. Also, think about the difficult times or hardships you have encountered that have stopped you from achieving your dreams. The purpose of looking at the bad times is so they can inspire you to realize what you want to improve. Set a timer and write down your ideas.

How do you know if it's your intuition talking to you? Well, just listen to the first thoughts that pop into your head and write them down. It's that simple. By focusing on those first thoughts, you listen to your inner self. By writing them down, you can become aware of and communicate with these thoughts for more desirable outcomes in your life.

As you thought about your past, you probably discovered or reflected on the reasons why certain things went the way they did in your life, for better or for worse. To find the right *why* that will transform your future, it's critical that you clearly understand and document the *whys* of your past. The only way to create lasting change is to become one with your current self and find ways to move forward in the right direction.

As with every Mind Map, don't forget to note any themes from your ideas in your notebook.

TOP OF THE MOUNTAIN TIP

...Writing down what you want in life is a great way to get things out of your mind and into action. Be clear in your desires. You must set big dreams so big inspiration follows with them, you will need that for motivation down the road...

Mind Map #4: *What does my ideal life look like?*

Now, to find your deepest *why* for going after your goals, reflect on what you want out of life, not what you know or believe others want for you. Allow yourself to dream big. With your notebook and timer ready think about how you see your ideal life. In the center circle prompt write:

What does my ideal life look like?

Allow this brainstorm to be limitless. This reflection is the baseline for recording and building your life dreams. Maybe your dreams are related to your hobbies, physical fitness, financial security, career aspirations, spiritual connections, family legacy, or community outreach...the idea list goes on.

...If you are struggling with this, you can also think about what you don't like about your current situation. You will then consider what the opposite version is and start listing out those that resonate with the life you want to become...

Once you are done with this final Mind Map, look through all the work you have done so far across each Mind Map and determine if any common themes are coming out. Write down 3 to 5 common themes or topics that really speak to you on a clean sheet of paper in your notebook.

For example, do you have many items about your passion for art? family connections? career accomplishment? etc

Now Ask Yourself Why...5 Times

For this exercise, let's say your ideal life brainstorm revealed many themes surrounding the goal of being financially free. Below the short list of themes you created in your notebook, start a life purpose statement build-out exercise for one of the selected items in the 'BLANK' below.

"My life purpose is to... 'BLANK' and then add the word 'because'...

Example: *My life purpose is to be financially free because...*

Now, to fill in the second half of this statement, ask yourself *why* 5 times. Follow the example conversation below to help you understand the internal dialogue process. Each number is you asking yourself another why-based question on the answer you gave from the previous why.

1. If your why for changing your life is to "be financially free," why do you think this is the case?

Answer: I need the time away from a corporate 9 to 5 as well as the space to pursue painting full-time.

2. Why specifically do you want to pursue painting?

Answer: It's what makes me feel most at home and feeds my inner child. I am also driven by the way my art affects others and brings joy into their lives.

3. Why does this matter to you?

Answer: I ignored my instinct to pursue art for many years and wish I had ways to incorporate it more into my life. My current job doesn't inspire me, and I don't feel I am growing in a direction toward fulfillment.

4. Why is it time now to pursue art?

Answer: A recent scenario showed me that I'm not where I want to be in life and that I've been putting off this passion for too long. I see myself being successful as an artist, with enough money to paint what I want to paint rather than what I think will be popular.

5. Why don't you want to paint what's popular?

Answer: I want to be free to express myself without inhibitions so that I can use my art to inspire others.

There you have it! This is the train of thought that will truly inspire change—it converts the ideal into the real. To succeed in conquering your personal summits, you need a fire in your belly. It needs to be personal, and it must be meaningful. Now all you have to do is put them together:

My life purpose is to [something you want] because [why you want it].

Example: *My life purpose is to be financially free because I want to be free to express myself without inhibitions so that I can use my art to inspire others.*

This *finding your why* exercise should show you why *Personal Growth* is the first of the *4 Mountains of Success*. It's the primary, underlying desire we all want out of life, whether we know it or not.

Your Turn!

Try to come up with as many *why* statements as possible for a particular goal you want to achieve. Some examples of *why or purpose* statements could be:

- to help animals

- to afford a healthier body and lifestyle

- to travel the world and learn other cultures

- to build/buy a home

- to have a family

- to create career success

- to be able to contribute to a global cause

- to help others in the community

- to inspire the world in a specific way

- to live with joy and mindful purpose

Then, dive deeper into each statement by continuing to ask yourself why—5 times! The above items are just examples. It's your turn to go through those Mind Maps and pick out the things and themes that make sense for you. Build your *why* statements.

You will likely have a small handful of purpose statements that resonate with you after this exercise. Try to create *why* statements for each of the *4 Mountains of Success: Personal Growth, Financial Freedom, Career Success, and Community Impact*. I recommend keeping it to 3-5 in total. You can always change them as time goes on.

...To have the most success with implementing your life purpose statements record these on a vision board in your home and in your journal to review daily to set intentions for your day. There will be more on this in later chapters...

Some Mountains Are Harder to Climb Than Others

My *4 Areas of Success* were progressing well around the time my aerospace engineering career was beginning to unfold and I continued to find ways to breathe life into my art and music. Through my job, I had friends who were adventurous and inspired me to try new things. The most challenging of my mountains was my finances.

I didn't have much financial education. I didn't know that I had jumped head-first into the rat race straight out of college like countless others. I ignored my spending other than once a month or so. And even though all I knew about money was pretty much not to acquire interest-based debt, acquire it I did. I simply didn't have the tools to organize or manage my money at the time.

Finding My First *Why*

By my 4th year out of college, I moved into a 2-bedroom duplex house that was way more expensive than any place I had been in before (but how exciting! Look at all the space! And a garage! Wow!). My boyfriend and I were in the happy phase where you get excited about everything, and you want to live a lifestyle that you may not have the means to maintain.

Somewhere around the 5-year mark after college, my boyfriend and I started questioning what we were doing and what life had in store for us. We were beginning to realize that we would never be able to afford to get out of the rat race and out of paying rent.

We decided we wanted to own a home but didn't understand how to get a down payment for a house with our current money strategies. We knew we had to make a significant change, which would only come from learning, analysis, and action. So, in this discovery process, we each were beginning to trip into our first *why*.

What was my why?

Well, I didn't like my situation at the time and the trajectory I could see myself going down. I needed a change—and fast! I knew I wanted financial freedom to remove stress and unlock my passions in life. I wanted to grow in my career and explore what I could become. I wanted to accomplish my goals, outside of just my work goals and then set higher ones. I wanted to support my family members when they needed help, grow my friendships through shared experiences, and give back to my community.

After much reflection, I found out that my deepest *why* was **to find stability so I could continue to grow and find my true self.** This realization is what mobilized me to start my journey to financial freedom.

Your why will change over time, just make sure to check in quarterly and adjust as you need to.

What Will You Pack in Your Backpack?

 Over time, your *whys* will likely change, which is expected! Most importantly, you revisit your dreams and your life purpose statement for a particular goal whenever you feel lost.

You have now packed the first item in your backpack: **Your Deepest *why*.** Are you ready to make a significant change in your life to reach the peak of your first big goal? Are you prepared to spend some dedicated time planning a course for success?

Aside from your deepest *why*, you have two more mental tools to pack in your backpack before the journey begins.

Your Deepest *Why....DONE!*

A *Positive Growth Mindset*

Mind-Body-Spirit exercise

Re-centering the mind is a constant exercise, not a one-time event. You, my friend, are choosing to commit daily to your mental growth and build a plan for your life that sticks—and for this I applaud you! You will thank yourself when you're at the top of your goal, the one you perhaps once thought you'd never reach. In the next chapter, you will pack a *Positive Growth Mindset* into your backpack—the second mental requirement for success of any kind.

 ## Next Steps Before Moving On

1. Go to www.ConquerYourSummit.com/resources to download the worksheets you will need.

2. If you prefer using a physical workbook for these activities you can purchase the Conquer Your Summit companion workbook to follow along chapter by chapter.

3. Record your life purpose statement(s) in the *Summit Method* Worksheet's *Your Deepest Why* tab.

Chapter 2

A Positive Growth Mindset

You now know your *life purpose statement(s)* and a brainstorm of what dreams you might strive for. From this space of clarity, you are ready to leverage a positive mindset to create success in your life.

The next thing you are going to pack into your backpack is what I call *Positive Growth Mindset*. You will need this as you climb through your *4 Mountains of Success: Personal Growth, Financial Freedom, Career Success, and Community Impact*.

Facing the Facts is Easy with the Right Mental Tools

In this book, you will be asked to dig into your current state of life, which can bring up many emotions. Therefore, it is critical that you improve or strengthen your relationship with yourself by knowing your deep inner mind. It is in knowing yourself that you can anticipate and neutralize negativity like a pro. This centered energy is what will guide you through developing and conquering your *Mountain of Personal Growth*.

With the *Summit Method*, you will also need to open all your financial accounts and start locating the accurate data, good and bad, to record the current state of your finances when planning for the financial aspect of your success. If that makes you freeze up a bit, this is exactly why we are learning the mental tools first. As with any mountain, summiting your *Mountain of Financial Freedom* starts with a single step—so, don't worry. I'm going to show you exactly how to face the facts in a calm, collected manner.

The topic of money usually leads directly towards how you get that money or your income, also known as your career. Getting in touch with the mind will help you gain the clarity to know whether or not your career suits you for the long term. You will need to dive into your passions within how you make money to make sure what you do is sustainable in that it brings you joy. In summiting your *Mountain of Career Success*, you will look at where you are today in your career and where you'd like to be—even if it's somewhere entirely new.

To plan your ascent along your *Mountain of Community*, you will need to think about all the people that surround you in your life—your family, friends, and the community you belong to and live your life through. They are your support system and part of how you will continue to fuel your motivation as you grow. The mental blocks we have with other people sometimes get in the way. This is why the mind is the key to unlocking how we interact, serve, and maintain relationships with others.

 TOP OF THE MOUNTAIN TIP

...As you continue to read this book, I encourage you to connect with family and friends to have them join you on your journey. Have them pick up this book and follow along with you. The more accountability partners you have, the better your outcome will be...

Choose Your Preferred Mindset

We carry our mindset through every thought we think, every word we speak, and every action we take. It's always there. You can't avoid it. What *is* under your control is the mindset you *choose* to carry in your reactions throughout your day-to-day life. While there are many interpretations and teachings of *mindset*, the *Summit Method* is most concerned with the contrast between a *Fixed Mindset* and a *Positive Growth Mindset*.

Along my journey, I have experienced critical point after critical point in the development of my mindset. Over the past 10 years, there were many instances in which my thoughts had calcified into a *Fixed Mindset* that was causing me distress and I knew I had to change my perspective. I created the *Summit Method* so it will take less time for you than it did for me to create that shift.

It took a powerful force for me to realize I needed to practice being open-minded and carry a *Positive Growth Mindset*.

Living in an RV

As I mentioned in my story in the previous chapter, my partner and I were struggling to figure out how to reach the goals we had about our personal growth, finances, career aspirations, and community engagement. We had worked our way into understanding our *why* for the time being, but we needed a real plan to get to the finish line of our dreams.

To start, we needed to figure out how to get out of financial insecurity. The problem was that even when ideas and solutions were brought to the table, I had not learned how to grow in my mindset to embrace change.

I'll never forget the day my partner reluctantly asked me how I felt about moving into an RV and living on the streets.

"I'm sorry, what!?... Umm, no. End of discussion."

I had an extreme case of a *Fixed Mindset*. But my partner's idea was already out in the open, and there was no turning back. During this time in my life, if someone offered something that rubbed against the mental limitations I had placed on what was possible (or in this case, comfortable!), I tended to respond with an aggressive no, but after letting it simmer in the back of my mind for a few days or so, I would reconsider. Like a good stew that gets tastier with time, the insane idea of moving into an RV intrigued me the more it simmered.

The biggest thing I grappled with was going from a two-bedroom living situation with a garage to only a couple hundred square feet of living space on wheels. It was going to take something pretty radical to flip my mindset surrounding my possessions. I knew this idea of living in an RV was going to help us reach our goals though so I was willing to try.

What the heck am I going to do with all my stuff??! How can I part with all the memories and furnishings I've collected over the years??!

Then my partner introduced me to the philosophies of minimalism and utility. When I thought through the concepts he was trying to teach me, I decided I needed to be more open.

Everyone thinks of changing the world but no one thinks of changing himself. – Leo Tolstoy

Unlock Your Potential with an Open Mind

When I became willing to explore living in an RV and work through what the RV life would actually look like, I realized I didn't need to keep my couch, table, bookshelves, or other furniture. It would be difficult to move everything and put it into storage, and for what reason? We had no idea where our lives were taking us. I began to examine whether each item was valuable enough to keep and pay for it to remain in storage.

In most cases, it wasn't. The financial cost of keeping all my possessions meant a much bigger storage unit. From a different viewpoint, I realized my possessions could go to someone else and provide value to them instead of sitting in the dark for potentially years. To get down to the basics, I created two categories: direct utility and sentimental value. If it was going to go into the storage unit, it needed to have a real reason—it had to be something that couldn't be easily replaced or something that we would need access for use.

When it came to sentimental items, I was able to justify getting rid of them by taking photos and compiling them in digital memory books. I included just enough of a little blurb in each photo caption to lead me down memory lane.

I learned to change my mindset. Once my focus became finding utility, it was suddenly easy for me to part with a huge amount of the items I had been dragging along for years. Moving into an RV and living on the streets was the first significant lifestyle change along the climb to my success. Don't worry—I'm not asking you to throw out Grandma's quilt and join a tiny home community! I had to learn how to change my mindset before being able to summon the success that would ensue. I had to be ready for change, listen, and be open-minded about the ideas I was being led to.

This doesn't mean you blindly follow newfound concepts. You must center yourself to get out of a *Fixed Mindset*. Let's explore what that means and how to do it.

The Two Types of Mindsets

Fixed Mindset: A *Fixed Mindset* is thinking what you are now is all you can be, and there is no need for change or a way to change. You focus on things you are already good at and make decisions to protect that comfort. You are afraid of failure, so you ensure you never get to where loss could happen. You often interact as if you know everything and there is no need for change.

Positive Growth Mindset: A *Positive Growth Mindset* acknowledges all experiences as worthy of being learned from, regardless of the outcome. Failure is not a problem because you can learn something and grow into a more actualized version of yourself than before the failure. Choosing to be challenged, think beyond petty thoughts, and be humble and open-minded in the face of *"failure"* is much more valuable in the long run than only placing yourself where you know you're comfortable or know you'll win repeatedly without much effort at all.

The Power of the Mind

Mindset is *created* by one's philosophies and attitudes and grows with the influences of time. The keyword here is *created*. This means that mindset isn't just born out of thin air. There is a process to creating, building, and launching a mindset. You have the power to freely create your mindset anywhere, anytime, and with anyone.

Our minds are like a business (minus the paperwork, business laws, and taxes!). They need constant work, growth, planning, and focused execution to expand. Once a business is established, it changes, grows, and builds upon itself. It doesn't stay precisely how it was the day it was established. In fact, it better be changing if it wants to be successful in the long run! Your mindset is no different.

> **If you ever think you're losing control of a situation, just shift your mindset and watch your situation change.** – Dr. Amelia Rose

We Only Truly Exist in the Mind

The mind is what makes us human and allows us each our individuality. Your reality is the mind, and it's just that—yours! No one else can read your mind or know what you're thinking in there. You have an infinite sandbox to explore anything you ever wanted. Vividly imagining the version of life you want to experience is the first step to achieving it.

The power of the mind is no joke! It even can tear you down. If you don't spend the time to strengthen what I call the *Mindset Change Muscle*, it will be harder for you to adapt to obstacles that may come up along your journey.

... What is your mindset about changing your goals, lifestyle, money management, job, community, and more in life? If you feel lost, don't forget the definition of mindset. It's a created attitude. It's time to decide what kind of attitude you want. Write down how you currently feel, and then write down what you want to feel...

Your *Mindset Change Muscle*

We live in a society that embraces positive, success-driven stories. Many mental health systems have not grown enough to help us learn from a young age that it is okay to have complex, negative thoughts and give us the tools to work through them. Because of this, most of us have a weak *Mindset Change Muscle*.

Some of you might say, *"I don't know what you are talking about. I adapt to change quickly and have no problems with my mindset."* I hate to break it to you, but that is what a *Fixed Mindset* person would say. And that's okay, you can change. What matters is what mindset you ultimately develop based on how you respond to your initial reactions.

That may be you today, but you are reading this book right now so you can become the person of tomorrow. Someone with a *Positive Growth Mindset*.

Take this book, for example. Let me ask you a question: **When you pick up this book to read, what attitude does your mind have?**

Are you super jazzed, ready to learn, and accomplish your dreams?

Or...

Are you reluctant and dragging your feet even to read one more page?

To get something out of this book, you must assess and align your mindset toward reading. This concept applies to anything and everything throughout your life. When you come across something that makes you feel like the mountain you are climbing is too high for you to reach, remember it's all in your mind. You can push yourself to do incredible things when you learn the skills to change your mindset.

...Changing your mindset is being able to say to yourself every morning: "I am pumped to be increasing my knowledge, ready to unlock my potential, and positive that I will take something away from this book that can change my life!" Positive affirmations all the way! This will make you more successful in life...

My Fixed Mindset and My Passion for Music

I started writing music in 2012 as a singer-songwriter in the folk genre. I wrote over 45 songs in the first 10 years and loved every minute of creating art and sharing it with others.

When I started trying to play gigs, people would say, *"Hey, do you have an album I can listen to? I love your music."* I didn't have anything recorded, so every time I heard that I felt like a failure and decided I needed to stop doing gigs to plan and record my album.

When I found the process of recording an album to be overwhelming and expensive, I looked for all the reasons why I couldn't do it. I was convinced that it wasn't possible and that I would have to do it myself. I researched recording studios, the music industry, and what I needed to do to prepare for this experience, but I never once stepped into a studio, called someone, or tried to change my mindset.

I spent 8 years not doing gigs while building up equipment, recording by myself off and on, and trying to create music. Nothing I made was up to my standards as a one-woman recording project. I was motivated and excited every time I met a musician I could collaborate with, but I spent so much energy trying to pretend I was knowledgeable. I was too afraid to admit I needed help. Why? Because I was so embarrassed, scared to fail, and fixed in my mindset.

Owning Your Vulnerabilities

It's weird how when you give into the fear of not getting the trophy or being the best, you end up being your worst. A *Fixed Mindset* lets fear and emotion take control of your ability to be successful. If I had been open and honest about where I was, what I wanted to do, and my vulnerabilities, I would have had people excited to help me. 10 years had passed with zero to limited progress. I had a yearly goal of recording my album, but I never got there because of my mindset. I carried the weight of not wanting to fail, so I would never try.

After leaving the Aerospace industry, I took a month-long sabbatical to focus on opening my inner mind and changing my mindset. I worked on my ability to say, *"You know what? I am not a professional musician nor a trained guitarist, but that is okay. I will sign up to record with a recording studio, be upfront about who I am and what my skills are, and simply express what I want to accomplish."*

Because I was willing to go in with a *Positive Growth Mindset* and forget about being the best, my life was changed. I recorded my first professionally produced song! Once I had changed my mindset enough just to start the process, I was able to work toward the entire album.

The Mindset Exercise

In order to really make change you must practice. Here is a short exercise to get you started. Grab your notebook and take 5 minutes to think deeply about a time when you carried a *Fixed Mindset*.

1. Write down the memory at the top of the page.

2. Take that memory and think about what a *Positive Growth Mindset* could have done to change your outcome. Write down what the *Positive Growth Mindset* version of you would have done instead just below the memory.

Take a moment. Notice how by mentally placing the ideal *Positive Growth Mindset* version over the original *Fixed Mindset* memory, you have opened new possibilities.

As you continue this book and come across something like, *"Wow, I have a lot of debt!"* and you panic! I want you to take a deep breath and ask yourself what your newly exercised *Mindset Change Muscle* will do for you. With a *Positive Growth Mindset,* you can attain the motivation and power needed to overcome any obstacle. By simply getting curious about the new mindset that would be needed in place for you to reach your goals, you learn to take the above *"Wow, I have a lot of debt!"* into:

"I have more debt than I thought, but I am ready to learn the steps to minimize it. The amount of debt I have is equivalent to the opportunity for learning and growth I have ahead of me! I know it will be challenging, but I will see to it that I maintain a positive mindset throughout the process. I will continue to remember that I will get out of debt, and that feeling of freedom will make every challenge I face worthwhile."

A positive mindset can build a positive physical and mental structure for an amazing life. – Hormuzd Dossabhoy

Sometimes, your *Mindset Change Muscle* needs a gentle shove in the right direction to help you become open to the growth that is available to you in a given situation. You don't have to walk around all muscled out, attempting to manage your mindset with brute force. It's best to gently coach your mind, gradually, into adopting a *Positive Growth Mindset* surrounding the subject in question. That being said, when you are facing a particularly difficult situation or decision, doing this can be easier said than done as competing forces rush into your mind and cause distress. It's no wonder you can't think about growth in these moments—you're just trying to focus on not having a panic attack! Take a deep breath. Help is on its way!

Conquering the Worry Monster

 Worry is a horrid beast. It bounces off the walls, ready to pounce on anyone who will let it anywhere near them. If you feel the worry monster near, glaring with those *Fixed Mindset* eyes, bring the focus back to the cold, hard facts. Making data-driven decisions following an episode of worry works wonders in neutralizing the frenzied state. It's my favorite hack for activating the *Mindset Change Muscle*. Upon gathering the data, analyzing the situation, and making a decision, you combat worry with logic. It is imperative, however, that you take the time to gather the facts, which is one of the things most people forget to do. Facts will set you free. Let's go through an example.

Let's say you find a mysterious spot on your skin and immediately panic because you jump to the conclusion that you have skin cancer. Well, gather the data. You don't know you have skin cancer until you visit the doctor and get tested. Only when it is confirmed that you have skin cancer can you analyze the options for what to do with your doctor. You must practice limiting worrying about it until you receive confirmation that your fears are real—but even then there are still more facts to gather. You and your doctor will create a plan and act on that plan. In sticking to the facts, the worry can melt away, you become more effective and constructive at solving the issue.

Now, of course, not all situations magically get better and get fixed but you get the point. It's about gathering facts and trying not to worry along the way.

Using the example above, let's say you can't get to the doctor for a whole week. Take a deep breath and know you are already doing a great job because you are gathering the data and have an appointment booked. You can do nothing more, so release your worry, and stop obsessively googling for answers. I know it's easier said than done, but you must try!

Along your *Summit Method* journey, you will find that the mind, body, and soul are deeply connected, and that worry is a toxic emotion. Worry leads to stress, which has a very real, physical effect on the body, so it has the potential to worsen your condition or at the very least cloud your judgment.

Yes, it's still scary, but sticking to the facts minimizes worry. We must manage our emotional state surrounding any given situation because it deals with how we experience it and can often make a situation worse if it goes unchecked. Having the mindset skills to manage your attitude will elevate the way you experience life, no matter what challenges you face.

What Are You Packing in Your Bag This Time?

You need your *Positive Growth Mindset* handy for the journey ahead, so pack that in your backpack right on top of your deepest why. To cultivate your *Positive Growth Mindset* skills, remember to listen to your inner thoughts. Allow your subconscious to unleash your creativity to imagine all the possibilities that are available to you within a given scenario.

...Successful people take their inner thoughts, dreams, and desires...record them...and keep them at the forefront of their minds. Then they make a PLAN to achieve them....

In the next chapter, I introduce your next tool: the *Mind-Body-Spirit exercise*. This is the final item to pack into your backpack before you're ready to start hiking to Base Camp to stop and plan the details of your life plan. It will be fun and easy from here on out because you are now *Positive Growth Minded* and excited about your future potential!

Next Steps Before Moving On

1. In your notebook, create two statements:

   ○ A *Positive Growth Mindset* sentence focused on the *4 Mountains of Success: Personal Growth, Financial Freedom, Career Success, and Community Impact.* This is to attune to and commit to the journey of conquering these mountains in your own life. In your own words, *why is it important for you to address these areas, and what mindset are you open to having upon beginning the trek?*

   ○ A statement regarding your definition of success. On this page, define what success means to you. This definition will shape the adventure that is to come.

2. If you are using the Conquer Your Summit workbook proceed to this same chapter number in the book to fill out the information.

Chapter 3
Harmony of Mind-Body-Spirit

**Your mind, emotions and body are instruments and the way
you align and tune them determines how well you play life.**
– Harbhajan Singh Yogi

Thus far on your journey to reach success, you've acquired *your deepest why*,
along with an unwaveringly *Positive Growth Mindset*. Now all you need is regular
check-ins with your mind, body, and spirit. This next mental tool is an exercise
you can do from anywhere, anytime, with anyone, and is designed to help you
reset your state of being when you need it most. It was created to support your
Mindset Change Muscle through challenging circumstances and situations.

The Check-in That Changed It All for Me

I used to get into negative spirals and arguments with others more often than I'd
like to admit. We all do. Nobody is perfect.

My husband came to me one day and said, *"Aliki, I would like you to try a
Mind-Body-Spirit exercise with me and see if it can connect us to a different mood
or mindset."* I looked at him with a questioning face wondering what new thing
he could be sharing with me now. He always enjoys bringing new thoughts and
ideas to the table which can be very fun and sometimes challenging.

I gave a little sigh and smiled. I had grown to realize that my life partner was always
there to show me new pathways that generally always made things better, so I was
ready.

He said:

"I want you to take a moment and pause. Take a deep breath and ask yourself how your mind, body, and spirit are feeling right now in this exact moment. Think about them one by one. I'll do it too, and then we each share our answers out loud with each other."

It seemed relatively simple, so I was open to it. *Here we go... Deep breath...*

My mind was worried. It was racing about the day's tasks and felt very cluttered.

My body felt well, and it was great to take a moment to have gratitude for being in good condition. People tend to only become aware of their bodies when they have aches and pains to focus on. It's good to recognize when the body is performing well too. I remembered at that moment that I had control over my body. I needed to be mindful of taking care of myself.

My spirit was caged and wanted to be free. I wanted to be happy and share that energy with others.

When isolating all 3, it was clear to me that my mind was running the show and it was dominating my body and spirit—almost bullying them! My spiraling worry had built up so much momentum that it was affecting my entire being. Yikes!

The mind is amazingly complex. It can contemplate many things simultaneously. The mind lives in the past and remembers all the details of importance but also lives in the future, calculating and concluding outcomes. It has the power to paralyze you with fear and worry but also to bring you peace. The mind is good at its job: *being a great analytical tool for future planning and risk avoidance.* It can be a pretty depressing job for the mind, though, as the tasks of future planning and risk avoidance usually involve looking at the problems of the past. But once you, the willing *Summit Method* mountaineer, become aware of this tendency and actively keep it in check, you can use the mind's talents to your advantage.

The mind-body connection is incredibly powerful. The mind can influence aches and pains by simply believing such pains are healed. But the body also needs to be taken care of. It requires the right fuel of healthy foods, proper rest, and methods to care for the mind. Have gratitude for your body regardless of its condition, and feed it with the mental energy to grow past any adverse ailments you may have.

The spirit is your connection to your magic, your power, and your intuition. You must have a clear pathway to access the voice of the subconscious to be 100% real with yourself. Your innermost feelings and desires express themselves, moving from your inner landscape to the outside world, through feelings and words. It's important to practice feeling what your spirit is telling you at any given moment to make sure you're on the right track.

Changing Your Mind

 Whenever you feel you might be spiraling a bit in your mind, stop and take a moment to be present with yourself. Cut out the world's physical distractions and look inward to your mind, body, and spirit by taking a moment to close your eyes. Ask yourself:

1. **What is your mind thinking about or focused on?**

2. **How does your body feel right now?**

3. **What your spirit is telling you?**

TOP OF THE MOUNTAIN TIP

...This exercise is great to do out loud with another person, as part of the intention behind this exercise is to get better at sharing your inner feelings with others and practice speaking your truth. This will help you out of a fixed mindset or negative rut...

I encourage you to take this exercise a step further and turn it into a 10- to 15-minute meditation. Expand from just how you feel in that moment to reflecting on your week or month. If you want to, write it down in your journal for deeper discovery so you can watch your growth each time you do the exercise. We spend so much time buzzing around that we miss opportunities to reflect on ourselves. After your check-in, find things to be genuinely grateful for. Thank yourself for something—anything—even if it's small.

This exercise is great for strengthening your *Mindset Change Muscle* because you can become aware of any negative energy emanating from your mind, body, or spirit. You then get to acknowledge the negative presence and ask if it can change.

Mind – Body – Spirit: How can we substitute this negative response with a positive one?

This is the start of reprogramming your being to align with your goals. Now you try! Trust me, it's fun, easy, and a great way to pause and reconnect with life.

Mind-Body-Spirit Exercise

Read through this section before you close your eyes and do the exercise yourself.

*What is the mind preoccupied with most
right now?*

Describe it out loud. Expressing yourself out loud can be a healing experience because it doesn't allow your mind to race through the exercise. You must form words and think through them.

What does your body feel like right now?

Take a moment to scan your body from head to toe and feel any aches, pains, or good feelings. Does everything feel in working order? Describe what you feel out loud. Accept and connect with all pains and discoveries. You can focus on how to remedy those pains later, right now you are focusing on recognizing them. If you have no issues, take a moment to thank yourself and remember that how you feel is primarily impacted by how you care for yourself.

What does your spirit feel like right now?

This one can be deceiving because it's easy to confuse the mind with the spirit, but I have a little trick that can help. Look for the connection between your heart and your mind—that's your spirit – how you feel in your heart. The mind can go back in time and jump into the future, but the spirit is always present. It is the passion that the heart beats for. When you center your mind on this topic, you train your mind to tap into the present and allow the spirit to speak to you. What is it telling you? Describe what you feel out loud. Don't discard it for being outrageous.

Now that you have read through the prompt, I want you to close your eyes and answer the questions about the status of your mind, body, and spirit. If you aren't in a place where you can talk out loud, that's okay; just make sure you try the exercise at some point in a space where you can.

TOP OF THE MOUNTAIN TIP

...Complete a Mind-Body-Spirit exercise once a week to bring gratitude and reflection into your life. This will keep you on the right course toward mental clarity. BONUS! Do this exercise with your partner, family member, or friend to allow you to connect and create a bond between your minds, bodies, and spirits...

What Are You Packing in Your Bag This Time?

So far, you have completed packing 2 of the 3 items you need for starting your journey: *your deepest why* and your *Positive Growth Mindset*. The new item you are packing is your *Mind-Body-Spirit exercise* to recenter yourself in difficult situations.

I hope most of your journey of discovery and planning is inspiring and that you are naturally excited with positive energy. But let's face it: some days you might just not be feeling it. On other days, you might be triggered by what someone else said or did. These feelings hit on wounds that can sometimes derail our path to success. Before it gets to the point of destruction, check in with yourself.

Remember **your deepest *why***; it will give you the strength to pull through.

Maintain your **Positive Growth Mindset**; it will free you up to new possibilities.

Use your **Mind-Body-Spirit exercise** to take a pause and see what's going on under the surface to meet it head-on so it doesn't come out sideways later.

Your dreams are too important to leave up to chance. We are talking about your fulfillment here, your satisfaction with life—or lack thereof! There are proven ways to improve. Take what you've learned and implement it to unlock the path to your most tremendous potential. This method transformed my life. You, too, can get there. You, too, will conquer your summits!

And now, it's time to begin. We will meet at Base Camp in Part Two of this book. Base Camp is a crucial step for mountaineers to plan for their big climb. You, my friend, have quite the climb ahead of you!

 Next Steps Before Moving On

1. Go through one *Mind-Body-Spirit exercise*. Then, practice incorporating it into your daily life or at least once a week to check in with the progress you're making within yourself. This will help you maintain integrity in your actions. Whenever you find yourself fraught with negative feelings, use the *Mind-Body-Spirit exercise* to reset and get back on track.

2. If you are using the Conquer Your Summit workbook proceed to this same chapter number in the book to fill out the information.

Part One Summary

Let's look at the tools you have acquired thus far in preparation for your hike to Base Camp, the resting space where you will begin your journey. So far:

1. You have *your deepest why* for the journey.

2. You have developed a *Positive Growth Mindset* for your life planning activities and strengthened your *Mindset Change Muscle*.

3. You learned the *Mind-Body-Spirit exercise* to use (at least) weekly for a mental reset. Try to do it when you feel intense negative energy flowing in your mind before reacting. This pause is crucial to your journey to success.

Part Two

Base Camp

As human beings, we want so much out of life, yet we can't quite articulate what we want. This paradox keeps us in the same vicious cycle of not making any progress.

Being clear on your goal means knowing exactly what the goal is, putting pen to paper, and intending for that goal to happen.

Interestingly enough, many people *are* meeting at least some of their goals, but since they aren't tracking them, they don't know when or how they did it. Did it take a couple of weeks or 5 years? You need to know this to continue on a steady path! Or on the other hand, so much time has elapsed since they wrote it down (and didn't follow up!) that they forgot their goal and therefore didn't see it to completion.

How does the universe know what you want if you don't *tell it* what you want and when you want it? You can't just stand at the top of the mountain, shout it out to the world, and expect it to materialize instantly. All you have to do is start by putting your goal on paper and have a way of determining whether or not you're on track as you go along.

On the hike to Base Camp, the mountaineer has some time to think about the challenges they may encounter on the way up the mountain they wish to summit. In Part Two, you will learn the art of planning: the act of making your intentions known. I'll show you exactly how to plan the climb to each of your summits for the next 5 years. Proper planning neutralizes any limiting thoughts about the past. It will put you in control *today*, no matter where you are along your path. Embrace the power of writing down data and seeing your dream through with several milestones that are easy to measure. You can always reference your data, build upon it, and make adjustments as needed.

Chapter 4

The Power of Planning

An hour of planning can save you 10 hours of doing. – Dale Carnegie

After packing your backpack, you walk to the trailhead to start your hike up to Base Camp. This section will be the longest in your journey but the easiest on the uphill incline. You will pass through many familiar mountains that you recognize by the vegetation and animals you've seen before against the backdrop of beautiful, awe-inspiring views. You have plenty of time here to reflect on where you currently are in your life before you get into Base Camp.

There it is! The Trailhead!

You are passing through the most leisurely section of the hike: a meadow with shady but scant forest cover and the occasional kiss from the sun peaking out from above it. You hear the birds chirping to the universal beat of the forest. This evokes an inner smile. You take in the fresh, clear breeze with closed eyes, and with each breath, you become more and more invigorated and curious about what will come next. As you walk up a slightly elevated chunk of the earth, gravity makes you aware of the weight of your backpack, which fills you with a feeling of security; you know you have the necessary supplies to make this trek.

As you walk, you take out your notebook and read aloud the affirmations you have written for yourself.

Congratulations! You made it into the next phase, where you will begin making your plan to live *your* best life! Having learned about finding your purpose, correcting your mindset and tactics to reset yourself when you get lost or frustrated it will be easier for you to address where you are going in life from here on out. In this trek phase, have your notebook ready. You will also need a computer as we get deeper into the details.

> **There are dreamers and there are planners; the planners
> make their dreams come true.** – Edwin Louis Cole

Planning is Freedom

My partner and I were initially indecisive about whether to live in an RV or not. We were struggling to find a strong financial base and accomplish the personal growth we desired at the time. We researched how to buy a home, first-time home buyer programs, and different types of loans. I even took a course on the home buying process for first-time home buyers to get qualified. None of it mattered because we didn't have the cash for a down payment for anything in our area.

Unfortunately, we worked at an aerospace company jam smack in the middle of Silicon Valley California, making it impossible to own something near work. (The San Francisco Bay area was an impossible market for first-time buyers in the 2010s!) No matter which way we looked at it, we needed to figure out how to save money if we were going to change our financial situation. We also craved the freedom to live anywhere we wanted. After much contemplation, it was decided that we would take up the crazy idea and move into an RV to save money.

We bought an old 2003 white and blue Tioga 29-foot RV we saw on Craigslist, the kind with the over cab bed that sleeps 8. It was a good fit for 2 people to live in since it had more storage. It wasn't the ideal situation, but it would help reap better rewards down the line.

This strenuous process was an exercise in courage, mental fortitude, and personal growth. I sold all my furniture, even the pieces I loved. I packed away as little as possible and was ready to start this exciting new life. I had to use many mental tools from my backpack to get through this phase of our journey and I had to learn to let go of the things I had carried for many years. I eventually realized they didn't actually matter. We had boxes labeled *storage*, *RV*, *donation*, *trash*, and *sell*.

The goal was to have as little as possible go into the RV since it was obviously very small comparatively. We anticipated having a storage unit down the street so we could access things we might need, but everything else: purge!

We had the RV before we officially moved out of the duplex we were living in, so we were able to go on a couple of trips first—and it was amazing! These short trips helped us wrap our minds around full-time RV living and the opportunities it would bring. We would no longer live each day jumping into the hamster wheel with our heads down, waking up in the same spin, and going nowhere. It was time to wake up, jump out of that wheel, and take in the riches around us outside.

With this newfound freedom, we knew we needed to build a life plan for ourselves. After all, we weren't moving into an RV on the streets for fun—at least not entirely! We had a purpose, drive, and vision for success! We needed to explore our potential and determine exactly how we would get there. On a beautiful sunny Saturday morning, we packed up the RV with everything we needed to head out of town. We had determined that we needed to do a big 5-year planning session to make sure we stayed on our course throughout this transitional phase of our lives.

How the Summit Event Started

 We drove across the Santa Cruz Mountains, through tall pine and redwood trees that created a green winding tunnel. Once we broke through, we were welcomed by the shining sun and the vast deep blue Pacific Ocean along the scenic drive of California One. The further we went on that epic drive, the more we were humbled by life's beauty and filled with inspiration for the future. It was awe-inspiring, and we realized there was so much to live and experience beyond the dull walls we left back home. We sensed that this trip was the breakthrough we needed for our lives to evolve into exactly what we imagined them to be.

We eventually found our way to a lovely little offshoot of the road right up against the crashing ocean waves, crisp rocks, and tidepools gleaming in the sunbeams. It was breathtaking. We parked and determined that it was the perfect spot for giving ourselves the mental and physical space to make a plan!

We didn't know it at the time, but this trip laid the foundation for what would later become the *Summit Method* that would help us and countless others reach success. Our environment was the catalyst we needed to successfully accomplish the task of facing the facts of the current state of our lives and be in the relaxed state required to plan for our ideal future.

We got our supplies together, including computers, notebooks, sticky notes, and paper. We even had a little TV monitor and a cable we could plug into our computers to project what we wanted to show each other on the screen. It was the perfect setup: space to explore our ideas, outdoor time to clear our minds, and a kitchen to cook in! Wow! What a retreat!

We worked on setting up a planning framework for our *4 Mountains of Success—Personal Growth, Financial, Career, and Community*—the 4 pillars we determined that most people needed to feel a sense of holistic satisfaction. We recorded our current state within each area on our computers.

Once the data was collected, we could analyze it and spend time discussing our options, exploring our feelings, and working through our mindsets centered around each area. The retreat setting allowed us the freedom to do the work at a leisurely pace. Since we had taken the entire weekend to solely focus on what we intended to do with our lives, we could take much-needed breaks throughout the day for walks and other types of exploration to clear our heads.

We Are What Our Minds Are

Humans are very visual creatures. When a desire is born, we see it in our minds first. Because of this, documenting your visualizations of the future is vital to unlocking your progress. Harnessing the power of visualization will boost that progress, no matter what your goal is.

No one else can see your mind. No one else can even know what you are thinking. Only you know your mind and what's happening in there! Throughout your hike to Base Camp, allow your mind's eye to visualize down to the detail what you want your life to look like in the *4 Mountains of Success*. Don't be afraid to dream big.

That being said, as glorious as the mind's ability is to imagine ideal outcomes, let's be honest: it's fleeting. One second you are thinking about that burrito you had for lunch and all its cheesy goodness. The next, you notice your phone ringing, and you are debating whether to answer, and then—*Oh wait! Did I lock the door at home?* We are all over the place. Actively turning off the mind as it naturally wanders in whatever direction is a crucial skill to have along your *Summit Method* journey. Distractions impede the level of focus required to effectively visualize the next few years of your life the way you intend to experience them; luckily, you have those shiny new mental tools you acquired in Part One for this reason!

The mind's specialty is creating future plans, so let's celebrate what the mind can do for us. You will now learn to make a proper plan for the best life for the next 5 years, a skill that will prove useful for many years to come. Now, let's talk about how to make your visualizations real with the focus and concreteness of a solid plan.

What is a Plan?

A plan can be a bazillion different things. It can be a single sentence written on a napkin that you save in your wallet, a one-page executive summary, or even a full-blown multi-page written-out plan with every detail possible! When it comes to the *Summit Method*, a plan is a written document that carries the following:

1. The **current state** of a given facet of your life. (for example – personal growth goals like hobbies, financial status, job status, who your friends are, what family you are most connected with, etc)

2. The **projection of the future** within that facet. (the goals you have or want to grow to over time)

With the purchase of this book, you have access to the worksheet that will guide your success. You need this worksheet when you go through the step-by-step approach outlined in the next chapter. Get them ready now, though! Navigate to www.conqueryoursummit.com/resources to download them.

Let's explore 3 different types of plans and what each is intended to accomplish along your *Summit Method* journey:

- Five-Year Plan

- Two-Year Action Plan

- Quarterly Check-Ins

FIVE-YEAR PLAN

TWO-YEAR ACTION PLAN

QUARTERLY CHECK-IN

Only after you have these plans can you truly analyze your progress and better understand your personalized path to success over the next 5 years. Let's dive in!

Five-Year Plan

FIVE-YEAR PLAN

Your *Five-Year Plan* is the broadest view of where you want to land in 5 years. It includes the goals you would like to accomplish and the general quality of life you imagine for yourself and your surroundings. A *Five-Year Plan* is created by:

- Looking at your current state

- Asking yourself where you want to be in 5 years

- Plotting the points between now and then

Easy right? Well, if it were easy, everyone would do it and follow their plans to completion. In reality, five-year planning is elusive, and some say it is pointless. How do you know where you are going to be in 5 years? What's the point? You'll probably change it over 100 times between now and then, right?

If the plan doesn't work, change the plan. But never the goal.
– Unknown

Ah, Yes. The fixed mindset opinion against five-year plans. You may be right that your plan will change but that's ok! In fact, that is the point! I am constantly reviewing and updating my *Five-Year Plan* with *Quarterly Check-Ins*. This allows me to achieve my most ambitious dreams in life by focusing on smaller milestones along the way. It is a game of relinquishing control by not rushing the process but also taking actionable steps toward that goal in the meantime.

There are things you need to start planning out over 5 years. Otherwise, you will wake up in 10 years and realize you never made any steps to achieve your dreams. Some examples of goals that generally take years to achieve include:

- **Personal growth** goals like learning a new language or getting in the best shape of your life.

- **Financial goals** like saving up for a house or going from bad to good credit.

- **Career goals** like training to enter a new field or starting a business.

- **Community goals** such as cultivating long-term relationships with clients or solidifying your bond with family and friends through regular interactions. Another big one is family planning if you are looking to have children.

...Sometimes thinking about your age now and your age in five years can help with idea creation for your Five-Year Plan for the years in between. You can ask yourself if there is anything you wish to have accomplished during that age range...

You get to decide each year, month, and day if you are still interested in following that path or choosing another course. The objective of the *Five-Year Plan* is to pinpoint a goal in the future and understand roughly what it might take to get there. And there is usually more than one way to hike up a mountain, so don't hesitate to get creative here!

Something worth noting is that 5 years is not enough time for some things you want to do. This plan is just the beginning. Once you accomplish one dream, you will find a new mountain of success to climb. The point is to spend time thinking about your future and make plans to get there over the next 5 years.

...What's a long-term overall life goal you have for yourself? Something that maybe will take longer than 5 years to accomplish. Write 1-3 ideas down in your notebook for the planning phase coming up. These larger long-term goals are perfect to think about when planning for 5 years because likely there are mini steps you need to accomplish during these next 5 years to get to that long-term goal completion...

Two-Year Action Plan

TWO-YEAR ACTION PLAN

You will now need to take that *Five-Year Plan* and create a *Two-Year Action Plan* to go with it. A *Two-Year Action Plan* is a laid-out version of each month of the first 2 years of your *Five-Year Plan*. We start with 2 years because 5 years is way too long for us to think in that much detail, and 1 year is not enough to give you the insight you need to reach your long-term dreams.

Populating the *Two-Year Action Plan* is easy. For each success area, write down 1 or 2 tangible goals that should be happening each month which feed towards accomplishing the overarching 5-year goals. The following example will better illustrate what I mean:

Example 1: Let's say you wish to work towards a new title at the company you work at:

1. In your *Five-Year Plan* worksheet, you would write the name of the company and your current title in the column for the first month of your *Two-Year Action Plan*.

2. Next, find the column cell of the month you want to make the change and write your desired title there.

3. Between the first month and that goal month, list the same title (or any that occur in between) until you have successfully transitioned to the title of your choice.

4. Look through the rest of your 2 years and change titles if you have more goals.

How do you predict how long it will realistically take to move up the ladder? Well, just take a moment to think about it from a logical, data-driven perspective. There are many ways to create a plan for timing a career move using the power of statistics, estimations, and projections. Data and logic will set you free, my friend.

- You can look up the average rate at which people move up in your company.

- You can ask coworkers for advice.

- You can ask to have meetings with your manager to lay out what you would need to do to get to that title.

- You can find a mentor in your company who would be willing to help you.

- You can go on LinkedIn, search for people in your field, and just message them to ask how they obtained the title you wish to have. Mentors can move mountains in your life.

The process of filling out your *Two-Year Action Plan* might bring up all sorts of emotions when you become clear on the very real, very approachable smaller tasks that can lead up to your bigger dream.

- Fear that you won't be able to complete the tasks required.

- Fear of rejection along the way.

- A feeling of dread might begin to weigh you down the more you think about *actually doing* your first few tasks.

Remember to refer to your deepest *why*, switch on your *Personal Growth Mindset*, and use your *Mind-Spirit-Body exercise* to become aware of and center how you are feeling. Change your negative feelings into actions! Intend on developing the courage to become who you want to be.

To become a manager at my first company, I was told I had to have 15 to 20 years of experience. I had about 3 at the time, but I was ready to lead and be the best manager I could be. Because of my hard work and dedication, I was promoted to management after only 6 years with the company!

With the right reason, mindset, and connection to yourself, you can defy the odds! The data is simply there to create a framework and healthy expectation of progress to keep you moving forward.

Let's look at another easy *Two-Year Action Plan* example:

Example 2: Let's say that one of your *Personal Growth* goals is to increase your squat power-lifting capabilities.

1. Input what weight you want to be able to squat each month as you gradually make your way to your larger, overarching goal.

2. Adjust your plan over time to reflect what has actually taken place in the gym. It's perfectly okay if it's not going as fast as you want it to. The point is to have a plan, try to reach it, and adjust accordingly.

3. Keep working towards your goal! You are already doing better than most people because you are giving yourself the best chance at success with the focus you are providing.

The *Two-Year Action Plan* has 2 commandments:

1. *Do not stop tracking.*

2. *Do not stop working toward your goal!*

If you get there before you expect to, great! If you're plateauing or going slower than you intended, just **keep using your mindset tools,** extend your plan, and make sure you record your data with regular check-ins. It's important to look at the data and ask yourself if there are any reasons you aren't making progress. Deep dive and determine any root cause distractions or issues in your life that you need to focus on getting rid of to open up your progress.

To help you succeed at using the *Two-Year Action Plan*, you're going to need to add one more planning tool to the mix.

Quarterly Check-Ins

Before you get to Base Camp where you will input all of your data into your plan, let's cut your *Two-Year Action Plan* in half. For this *Two-Year Action Plan* to work and for each month's tasks to have a rhyme and reason, you need to have goals for each year as well. You are probably thinking, "Oh, like New Year's resolutions!" Well, no. Let's be honest, how many people keep New Year's resolutions? Very few. Many don't even attempt their resolutions. Most fall off and forget them within a month or so. With the *Summit Method*, you will **accomplish** your yearly goals by splitting them up into quarterly goals—a goal for each 3-month quarter of the year.

It's natural for us to think in year chucks so you will still think of the year as a whole but set goals toward quarterly deadlines. These *Quarterly Goals* can be started regardless of the time of the year you are reading this book. Let's say it's currently August. That means you will set your *Quarterly Goals* starting in August for the remainder of that year but still have a check-in at the end of

September, which is when the third quarter of the year ends. You will then keep working on your goals for the final quarter leading into January, and so on.

When should you have *Quarterly Goals* set for a check-in?

- **Quarter 1: January February March** *(Plan for your Quarterly Check-in to be in the last week of March or the first week of April)*

- **Quarter 2: April May June** *(Plan for your Quarterly Check-in to be in the last week of June or the first week of July)*

- **Quarter 3: July August September** *(Plan for your Quarterly Check-in to be in the last week of September or the first week of October)*

- **Quarter 4: October November December** *(Plan for your Quarterly Check-in to be in the last week of December or the first week of January)*

These goals are slightly different from the others in the *Five-Year Plan* and *Two-Year Action Plan* because you will use the SMART goals methodology to create them. SMART stands for:

Specific   **M**easurable   **A**ttainable   **R**elevant   **T**ime-bound

You must know your goal, plan how to accomplish it, and declare when you need to get it done. You may have a goal to "lose weight" but a SMART goal iteration would be, "I will lose 20 pounds by May 1st by controlling my food intake and working out 3 days a week to become 150 pounds."

If you don't focus on *how* you plan to complete your goal, you will likely never actually work on completing it. Building a solid plan today will make for success tomorrow. *You got this!*

A goal without a plan is just a wish. – Antoine de
Saint-Exupéry

You can see Base Camp up in the distance—just one short stretch of the trail to go! After spending a much-needed break at the gorgeous alpine lake, you are ready to keep going.

Walking up from the lake, you run into a group of hikers on their way down from Base Camp. You are delighted to see other smiling faces and hear about their favorite

parts of the journey. With new information to look forward to on the hike, you feel the energy to keep pushing on. As you pass into an area covered in tall brush, you notice the sudden bustle of feathered, furry, and flying creatures.

You hear a screech from above and see a beautiful eagle soaring gracefully through the wind above you. You can't help but be humbled by the expanse around you, the plants, animals, and people coexisting within this beautiful trek up the mountain. You realize you aren't alone on your journey.

 ## Next Steps Before Moving On

1. Go to www.ConquerYourSummit.com/resources to download the worksheets you will need to follow along and track the current state of each *Mountain of Success* in the next few chapters!

2. If you are using the Conquer Your Summit workbook proceed to this same chapter number in the book to fill out the information.

Chapter 5

Your First Summit Event

You have made it to Base Camp! You hiked all the way up through the adventurous miles of the mountain terrain to get to this point. Base Camp is where you must spend ample time getting ready for the most strenuous parts of your journey up the mountain. Take all the time you need. Here you will acclimate to the environment and make sure you have done your final checks before taking the trek up to the top of your first mountain of planning.

Your Very Own Summit Event!

You now not only have the mental tools in your backpack, but you have also embodied the power of planning. You are ready for the actual act of setting your goals—your very first *Summit Event* (remember my retreat by the ocean?)! This check-in is a mandatory part of the work with an actual scheduled date, time, agenda, and process flow.

During your *Summit Event*, you will fill out a worksheet about the current state of your *Personal Growth, Financial Freedom, Career Success, and Community Impact.* You will look at where you're at currently in each area and where you want to go!

Your *Summit Event* is simple but powerful. It's when you set aside your daily life obligations and focus on brainstorming, analyzing, and filling out your life planning tools. Later on, the *Summit Event* becomes where you jump back into those plans, and you check in on your progress to update your plans.

Will this framework change? Of course! Each time you do your *Summit Event*, it will be a new liberating experience of deciding where you will go next. You might be verifying you are still on target for your goals, correcting your course, or plotting a new trail to a different mountain in life. This is perfectly okay, and in fact, it's part of the process! You can't make your plans perfect, and you can't be married to them. The goal of the *Summit Event* is to spend time mapping out how you, at this moment, see yourself growing, changing, and breaking down barriers to accomplish your life goals. It is merely a directional heading with ways to gauge your progress. Even if it changes, another plan must replace it. Keep yourself accountable here because you are worth it. The essence of the *Summit Event* is to build a life you love—the life you deserve!

What's on the Agenda?

Let's dive into the intricacies of the *Summit Event* so you can plan successfully for yours. The *Summit Event* is centered around the following 5 elements:

1. **Retreat**: a 'vacation' to the location of your choice with just yourself or with your planning partner

2. **Ground Rules**: the *Summit Event* guidelines for committing to a *Positive Growth Mindset*

3. **Documentation**: the use of computers/paper/whiteboard/sticky notes throughout the planning process

4. **Fun**: taking effective mental breaks along the way

5. **Agenda**: adhering to the most conducive process for planning

Let's dive into each of these elements

Retreat: Your Mini-Vacation Away from the Hustle and Bustle of Life

 Finally, we have made it to the retreat! I just love that word, don't you? Just hearing it evokes the images and feelings of a peaceful weekend away.

When you remove the distractions of your day-to-day life and relax in a quiet, secluded place where you can submerge your mind, body, and spirit in a peaceful state, you are free to think thoughts that feed your soul and unleash the most potent parts of your mind.

Take a minute and daydream with me. Where would you want to go for a retreat if you could go anywhere? Is it the ocean where you can hear the crashing waves and the seabirds' subtle coos? Is it a quiet forest of soaring trees, a backyard bungalow, alpine lakes, or crisp desert openness? Can you tell I'm a nature lover? These are all my types of retreats, but you don't need to be out in nature to retreat. I want you to close your eyes and visualize *your* ideal retreat location.

To start your *Summit Event*, consider your dream retreat and figure out what you can do to actually accomplish your setup. Keep that ideal retreat feeling with you as you find the most realistic version of it that you can create for this first try.

 TOP OF THE MOUNTAIN TIP *…Try to avoid doing your first Summit Event at home. If you can, find a place that is not connected to your normal everyday life. Doing this will help you get out of your current mindset and give rise to the future version of yourself. It will also eliminate the distractions you may have at home (items, people, noises, thoughts, your long to-do list!)…*

You will need to be able to connect to the internet to dive deep into your data and access your current state files. There are ways to download the files and work

offline if you really want to, but you need to make sure you did everything that's needed to document your current state before you go off on your retreat if you choose a destination with no internet connection. You won't be able to look up your bank accounts in the wild without Wi-Fi! Just be sure you think through your location the best you can and, at a minimum, have cell service.

 If you believe there is no way you can go anywhere else but stay at home, then I want you to think outside the box. I want you to try your hardest to set up a room, outdoor space, or area where you can make your super unique *Summit Event* space. Maybe move some furniture around to make it feel different or temporarily bring in some art, color, or plants near the area. You can even incorporate some scents such as candles or incense and adjust the lighting to create a different mood. This may sound silly, but the act of creating a sacred space that communicates to the subconscious that *this is important* will significantly benefit your progress.

You want to enter this space with peace, calm, and a passion for doing great things. I know you can do this! Take some time to brainstorm where you might be able to go outside of your home or how you can change your home up for this exercise. Feel free to write any notes in your notebook before we move on.

Do you need to start doing an epic retreat every 3 months to perform the *Summit Method*? Not unless you really want to! The step of scheduling and planning your first *Summit Event* is designed to encourage you to incorporate the retreat aspect of the work at least the first time.

I want you to consider this a mini vacation away from your current life. You are choosing to do something that is going to open your future. After that point, when you start getting the hang of your plans and check-ins, you can find ways to hold your *Summit Event* that doesn't need to be a big retreat and can fit into your regular routine.

I find that taking time away is always a healthy reset. I strongly encourage you to figure out how to do something like one vacation-style retreat at least yearly and then perhaps do the other 3 check-ins in the year at home.

Completing Your Summit Event Independently

I want to reiterate that the *Summit Event* is for everyone. You can mold it to what you need.

You can do this event individually or with a partner.

That being said, you will get different things out of this depending on if you are doing it alone or with someone else. Neither is the correct way; you should just decide how you want to experience your *Summit Event* and get started. You can always do it again with a partner after you have your own.

If you do this alone, the benefits are that you will be incredibly focused on yourself, where you are, and where you want to be without distractions or tugs from someone else's life. You may have a significant other but still choose to do the *Summit Event* yourself. That is totally okay. At the end of the day, what matters most is that you are sitting down and making your plan, taking the time needed to create your path to conquer your summits!

Completing Your Summit Event with a Partner

When you follow the *Summit Event* with a partner, whether romantic or platonic, you will find yourself opening up differently. You might be saying, "How does this work? Wouldn't doing this activity, which reveals your deepest thoughts, be more difficult with another person around?"

Yes, in some cases. However, because of the mental skills we put into our backpacks at the beginning of the book, we should be able to overcome this mental block. You should feel comfortable in this space with other people by having a *Positive Growth Mindset* and following the *Ground Rules* of the *Summit Event* (which we will discuss shortly!).

The value that other people provide in this exercise is that they can help you ask the tough questions that need to be asked and can provide you with additional thoughts and advice. Collaboration is a beautiful thing. You will learn things about yourself and your partner that will improve your relationship and challenge you to become a more self-actualized person.

So, take a moment and think about if you will do this with yourself or a partner. I highly recommend doing this with a significant other if you have been together a long while. You can also do your *Summit Event* with an accountability partner, such as a best friend, sibling, or parent.

When we first created the *Summit Event*, my husband and I wanted to make sure we built our own answers to life first before working as a team. We separated off with our laptops and made stabs at creating worksheets from scratch by ourselves first. We set timers for chunks of focus time and then came back together to share what we did. It was very enlightening!

We learned things about each other we didn't know before. We became aware of what we were currently doing, and we were excited about what was to come. In these moments, we realized something bigger was going on than just creating a 2 to 5-year plan. We were learning how to create a strategy that would allow us to support each other in making our dreams actually happen.

It wasn't all business, either! Since we were in a retreat environment, we were able to go for short walks on the beach, hike in the hills or just relax in the sun for a bit. It was critical to jump out of the physical planning space multiple times between the exercises we were doing to stay mentally focused on our *Summit Event*.

We continued working by collecting our information individually and then coming together for each area of success to compare, collaborate, change, and grow. Once we had a pretty reasonable plan, it was incredibly freeing.

I couldn't believe it! We did it, and it was so easy to do. We created a simple framework for how to look at our life and now just needed to execute it.

Ground Rules: Staying Connected to Your Positive Growth Mindset

For your *Summit Event*, there are some basic rules to follow—*Ground Rules*. They are the bedrock of your experience. Without them, you will be less engaged and quick to jump into the negative, *Fixed Mindset* spaces of your mind in which you are less effective.

When you get to your *Summit Event* destination, you must stick to the *Ground Rules* for the best results. *Ground Rules* may seem like something you don't need if you are doing this alone. Nope! Even *you* need *Ground Rules* because you have many other people and voices in your head trying to tell you what to do. You need to keep these influences in check! When working with a partner, the *Ground Rules* help you interact human to human and reduce potential conflicts. Read the *Ground Rules*, write or type and print them out, set them up beside you throughout the process, and follow them!

The Ground Rules of the Summit Event

Rules for everyone:

> 1. No cell phones out. Use a computer if you need to look something up.
>
> 2. Support your thoughts and passions. Don't underestimate yourself.
>
> 3. Focus. Do one thing at a time.
>
> 4. Schedule frequent breaks.

And if your Summit Event is completed with a partner, add these to the list:

> 1. Remember to actively listen to your partner.
>
> 2. Support each other's thoughts and ideas, regardless of your personal feelings.
>
> 3. Remove biases when communicating with each other.

...If these topics trigger any difficult emotions and you become frustrated...Stop... Voice what you're feeling out loud and perform the Mind-Body-Spirit exercise until you have reset your state of being and continue the process. It will all be worth it in the end! You'll see!...

Documentation: The Importance of Recording Your Process

Use the worksheet provided to assess the current state of where you are today. Then, sprinkle the ideas you might have for big goals plotted in the *future* columns. You can download the file and work offline if you need to, or you can pull up your web browser and keep inputting the plan directly into the sheet.

I did my first *Summit Event* as an oceanside retreat in an RV with no cell phone service. I had a small TV that I could plug my computer into, a dining table, my laptop, and my cell phone (to tether to the internet). I also cleared the wall space area so I could display my sticky notes.

It was essential to have a pile of plain white paper and colored pens for drawing, mind mapping, and taking notes as required. For you, this could all take place in your notebook—it doesn't have to be a separate stack of papers.

...We found that the TV monitor helped us with the sharing portion of the journey. I would highly recommend it! It allowed us to display each other's plans when we were reviewing data or presenting information to each other. This way, we could both see clearly, and we didn't have to try to huddle around a small laptop screen!...

Fun: Release Your Mind by Honoring Your Breaks

Like any task that requires energy, you will need regular breaks along the way. If you start your *Summit Event* and just power through it, a few things will likely happen:

- You will have a miserable experience.

- Your mind will become uneasy and you will be quick to quit.

- You will leave your *Summit Event* never wanting to do it again.

- You might end up saying things/thinking things you don't actually mean that simply stem from frustration that could have been avoided.

The mind is a crazy place. It needs nurturing. So, please follow the structure, incorporate joy into this process, and make room for fun!

The goal is to have an amazing event that will springboard you toward a more extraordinary life! How do you do this? Well, there is an agenda for your *Summit Event* that provides a reasonable amount of time for planning, breaks, fun, fuel, and, most importantly, celebration! After all, it is a pretty big deal that you decided to take time out of your everyday life to focus on yourself. Once you have completed your *Summit Event*, you deserve more than just a pat on the back. You deserve a celebration!

 ...If you work out extra hard, you are going to get sore. If you eat right and stretch after working out, you will progress towards your fitness goals faster because you spent time caring for those muscles. It's the same with the Summit Event. You must take breaks to free your mind and be the most excellent version of yourself when it's time to focus again...

The Summit Event Agenda

 If working with a partner, set the agenda together and agree on it. Depending on when you start the day, you must modify the template agenda to incorporate your needs for breakfast, lunch, and/or dinner. Go to the agenda tab of your *Summit Method* worksheet to edit. Feel free to make any changes you need to, but if you haven't done this before, you might want to follow the set agenda and make tweaks as needed.

Example from the *Summit Method* template: *(Full agenda with example times listed that can be changed to meet your needs)*

09:00 – 09:30 **30 Minutes** Briefly review your current state plan to make sure it's all filled out and share it with your partner if you have not already done so.

Note: You must determine the current state of each Mountain of Success before starting your Summit Event. I will show you exactly how to do this in Part Three! You should budget about an hour or two for this task to be completed before the event.

09:30 – 11:00 **1.5 Hours** Populate your *Five-Year Plan* by yourself.

11:00 – 11:15 **15 Minutes** Break time!

11:15 – 12:15 **1 Hour** Share your *Five-Year Plan* with your partner. Move to the next task if you are doing the event individually. You might have to adjust times to make sense for your day when removing the partner check-in items.

Note: Adjust your plans now that you know each other's individual goals for the Five-Year Plan. Learn more about each other in this exercise & support each other's dreams

12:15 – 01:00 **45 Minutes** Break time! (Maybe lunch!)

01:00 – 02:00 **1 Hour**   Develop your *Two-Year Action Plan* by yourself.

02:00 – 02:30 **30 Minutes** Share your *Two-Year Action Plan* with your partner.

Note: Adjust your plans now that you know each other's individual goals for the Two-Year Action Plan. Learn more about each other in this exercise & support each other's dreams.

02:30 – 02:45 **15 Minutes** Break time!

02:45 – 03:15 **30 Minutes** Decide your *Quarterly SMART Goals* by yourself.

03:15 – 03:45 **30 Minutes** Share your *Quarterly SMART Goals* with your partner.

Note: Adjust your plans now that you know each other's individual goals for your Quarterly Check-Ins. Learn more about each other in this exercise & support each other's dreams.

03:45 – 04:00 **15 Minutes** Post these goals somewhere you will see them regularly.

04:00 – 04:15 **15 Minutes** Schedule your next *Summit Event*!

Before you end, make sure you actually put that next Summit Event in your calendar and review the plans you made during the event. Start taking some actions toward what you are going to do in the first 3 months after your Summit Event.

04:15- ?   **Length of choice**   Schedule another day of planning if required. If you're all set, it's time to celebrate!

Celebration!

 It's time to congratulate yourself on the completion of your *Summit Event*! Pick a fun way to celebrate your success and give yourself a round of applause! Reward yourself for doing something that will make your life better.

As you go through your first *Summit Event*, take note of what you did and the timeframes you needed to accomplish them. You can always tailor the agenda to your own needs. Over time, you will find that your *Summit Event* will naturally evolve as you strengthen all your planning muscles.

In Part Three, we will dive into the prep work required for your *Summit Event* (all the things you need for that first activity on the agenda!). This is where things are going to get messy—in a good way. You have all those papers, sticky notes, computers, and supplies because you aren't just going to sit down and start magically typing a perfect plan into the worksheet. You will need a way to organize random thoughts into logical patterns, and you can accomplish that with your different papers and tools, like a mad scientist of life planning.

If you are ready to dive into the content of this book to live your best life but feel like you could use some extra help to get there, visit www.ConquerYourSummit.com/coaching.

 ## Next Steps Before Moving On

1. Open your notebook and go back to the Mind Maps we did in Part One. Write down the most important aspirations for each of your *4 Mountains of Success: Personal Growth, Financial Freedom, Career Success, and Community Impact.*

2. If you are using the Conquer Your Summit workbook proceed to this same chapter number in the book to fill out the information.

3. Before jumping into action and doing your *Summit Event*, jot down some notes in your notebook as you read the next few chapters. If something resonates and you want to remember it, write it down for when you actually start your event.

Part Two Summary

You have successfully made use of your time at Base Camp! You learned:

1. The fundamentals behind the types of plans you are going to create and manage: a *Five-Year Plan*, a *Two-Year Action Plan*, and *Quarterly Goals*.

2. All about the *Summit Event* and got ideas for how to execute it.

Are you excited about your own personal retreat that doubles as a productive life-changing experience? I'm super excited *for* you!

FIVE-YEAR PLAN

TWO-YEAR ACTION PLAN

QUARTERLY GOALS

Part Three is where you will zoom into each of your *Mountains of Success* and get a feel for the current state of your life as a whole. This will better equip you for your journey to self-fulfillment!

Part Three

The View of Your Mountain Range: The 4 Areas of Success

A person must feel they are in a good place with themselves, their resources, their path to gathering resources in the future, and their relationships with others to be self-actualized. Maslow's Hierarchy of Needs would have these qualifications organized in order of importance, but with the *Summit Method*, we are improving simultaneously in all 4 *Mountains of Success*.

Chapter 6 is dedicated to discovering where you stand with your *Mountain of Personal Growth*.

Chapter 7 is dedicated to understanding your current state for your *Mountain of Financial Freedom*.

Chapter 8 is dedicated to documenting the now around your *Mountain of* **Career Success**.

Chapter 9 is dedicated to wrapping up who is important right now for your *Mountain of* **Community Impact**.

By tracking each area at the same time, we ensure we are making progress in life in a balanced manner so that no *one* area of life is sacrificed for another. Part Three is all about the idiosyncrasies of each of your mountains. Each climb may differ, but the process is the same. The *Summit Method* is your straightforward guide to making any dream come true! You *can* have it all, and this is how you will make sure you do.

Charting Your Course

At the end of each chapter in Part Three, open the *Five-Year Plan* worksheet and fill out the information you gather on the *Current Assessment* tab under its respective category: *Personal Growth, Financial Freedom, Career Success,* or *Community Impact.*

Chapter 6

The Mountain of Personal Growth

What you get by achieving your goals is not as important as what you become by achieving your goals. – Zig Ziglar

You have found the shady trees and forest streams to be the most peaceful part of the hike. As the forest thins into a new clearing, you notice more sun on the path. The trail is starting to become scattered, with larger rocks on one side leading down a mountain with a meadow to the other side. Wildflowers are sprouting up in every possible crevice, swaying in the breeze. You are amazed at the diversity of life, the colors through the field, and the life around you.

 This first mountain is one you choose to just enjoy the views with a less strenuous climb. As you turn up on the last switchback up the meadow side of the mountain, your eyes are delighted to gaze upon a small alpine lake. Its crystal-clear water reflecting the other mountain peaks above is breathtaking. There is so much to see in this hike segment, and you genuinely feel awe-inspired by what nature can create.

Who are *you*? What makes *you* happy? What do *you* want out of life? In this chapter, you get to explore yourself—the most unique, incredible person you know! Here you can uncover your most profound dreams, goals, and passions. You will use the information in this chapter to populate your *Current Assessment* for *Personal Growth* and then save the items you are looking to in the future for the *Five-Year Plan* part that comes up next in later chapters.

Climbing with a Buddy – Note, if you are completing the *Summit Method* with a partner, this is the time when the 2 of you will bring your independent plans together and learn more about the other person. You will grow in your relationship and become closer if you then figure out how to create a collective plan together that will support both your dreams and goals. You might also realize a dream you have doesn't make sense when you compare it against your partner's plan. Dive deeper into that. Ask the hard questions to each other on why that is. Is there something the 2 of you need to work on in your relationship to grow to support each other better?

Master Growth Through Multiple Ambitions

My goals tend to multiply. This can be very exciting but also exhausting. It requires me to make sure that I remember my priorities and put as much focus into my planning as possible.

In no particular order, I want to be a touring musician, best-selling book author, muralist, world traveler, successful business owner, fit athlete, beach-going retiree, and a mother to incredible children someday.

I want you to also jump into as many ambitions as you can so you can grow from them and become the best possible version of yourself.

A Campfire Story About Personal Growth

A close friend of mine was in university during the most defining years of his growth into adulthood. While studying to become a Mechanical Engineer, he could not get into classes he needed which in compacted majors can set you back years in your graduation timeline. This was unacceptable, and he had a big decision to make. Drop out of college, jump into a new path, or stay the course like everyone else.

Sometimes, you must take giant leaps to make the most significant difference in your life and grow to the highest potential. In this case, he chose to leave that university and move to an entirely new city to start over. Here he focused on a city college program to learn a trade skill in becoming an auto mechanic that would allow him to get a higher-paying job part-time than a restaurant. Once he had that running, he could apply to a different local university to complete his original goal of completing his bachelor's degree in engineering.

He achieved a higher level of independence and achievement by making the hardest decision to quit his first university. Only then could he unlock the new growth that led him to the realization to study Manufacturing Engineering and grow his career from there. Sometimes in life, you have to take the big leaps for big rewards.

...Personal growth is not just about setting a goal and working on a plan to accomplish it. To truly grow as a person, you need to focus on what you are learning about yourself along the way...

Just Keep Checking In

The most important part of *Personal Growth* is overcoming obstacles, knowledge gaps, and complacency. If you are complacent, you will never achieve your goals. You must dive deeply into who you are, who you want to be, and what you might need to bring forward to rekindle your drive and motivation.

I am always working on making progress in all my passions in one way or another because I have laid out a plan. I have worked on my *Personal Growth* goals my whole life. Reaching the top of this mountain takes time, dedication, and a *Positive Growth Mindse*t.

Once you reach a higher altitude, it can feel like the path never ends and you might never reach that flag at the top of the mountain, but if you stick with your plan, you are sure to succeed. Once you reach the top of one mountain, you will feel so exhilarated that you'll start planning your next mountain climb almost immediately. You'll find that it's not the summit, but rather the climb that feeds your soul.

... The key to mastering your ambitions is to complete a Mind Map to help you gather a list of 100 things you want to accomplish in life. You will have a few that are center stage in your life, as well as a collection of back burner items, but you need to keep referencing those back burner items because you never know when they might jump to the top of your list...

Your Personal Growth Mind Map

It's Mind Map time! Let's brainstorm what you wish to receive from your *Personal Growth* journey.

Mind Map #5: *What do I want my Personal Growth throughout life to look like?*

Grab your notebook. Set a 5-minute timer and think about how you see your ideal life. The center circle prompt is: *What Personal Growth goals do I have for myself?*

Now, brain-dump anything you can think of that you ever wanted out of life. Think of the past, present, and the future. Focus on getting as much content and ideas on the page as possible because *every idea is good*. Nothing is crazy. What's crazy is if you choose to limit yourself without even trying to make a plan to accomplish it. You've got to give yourself a fighting chance!

Think about ideas around personal accomplishments, hobbies, fitness, big events, education, volunteer work, spirituality, meditation, etc. Feel free to wander into other areas of success within finances, jobs, or family-related things, even though you will develop separate dedicated plans for those coming up. Open your mind to anything you can possibly think of that you want out of life. Big, small. Short term, long term. Retirement. Just think about you and your whole life ahead of you. What are the *Personal Growth* goals you would like to set for yourself?

If you need more time, take another 5 minutes.

Now what?

Once you have completed your Mind Map, take those items and group them into similar categories or themes. Doing this grouping will help you refine your goals and help you determine if an item should be a goal of its own, be joined with another overarching goal, or even be on the list at all.

Let's say you notice that you have multiple items related to health. Circle each of them with a colored marker. Keep looking for things within a similar theme and make sure you star or color them differently. Ultimately, it should be easy to both see your different themes come to life and pinpoint the stragglers.

The point of doing this is to help you realize which *Personal Growth* goals are most important to you. If a bunch of things centered around the same thing keeps popping up for you, you need to make sure you focus on those when creating your *Quarterly Goals*.

Consider Time

Now, on a new sheet of paper in your notebook, write columns: *now*, *future*, and *maybe someday*.

Under each column list which goal goes in which time slot.

Now: Actively doing now or starting within the next month or so

Future: Items you know you must do down the road in your planning

Maybe Someday: Things you are passionate about but don't know how or when to fit in

You may find there are items from your original Mind Map that you didn't transfer over to your 3 buckets. I want you to ask yourself why. Why are you setting them aside? Make sure you have a good reason or at the minimum have spent time exploring what hinders you since there might be something you need to unlock to set yourself free. Spending life not working toward what truly serves your soul can be empty, so it's essential to ensure you don't back-burner your passions. Passion makes us happy, and happiness is how we fuel life.

Sharing Your Mind Map with a Partner

If you are doing this with a partner or friend, it's time for you to come together and share your Mind Maps. Here are some tips for executing this step successfully:

- Sharing your deepest passions with your partner can be tough, but remember to always refer to your *deepest why*, your *Positive Growth Mindset*, and your *Mind-Body-Spirit exercise* if you're having difficulty.

- Everyone participating in this climb should maintain an open mindset and be ready to listen to you share.

- Make sure you set expectations with each other before sharing. As you go through the ideas on your Mind Map and the timing chunks you categorized, you will find that some things might conflict when comparing plans. Let's say your partner wants to become a firefighter one day, and you are uncomfortable or nervous about that. This isn't the time to panic; it's the time to communicate. This is how you learn to start supporting each other's goals and make sure you find the needed middle ground in your relationships.

Once you have reviewed each other's individual Mind Maps do the following:

1. Grab another blank piece of paper and a timer.

2. Set the timer for 5 minutes and decide who will have the pen.

3. Together, verbally list your passions and goals that coincide with one another. Write down the easy, fun items first.

4. Then, separately list the tough conversations, such as whether or not to have children. Add more time if you need it. You don't have to have the conversation or make decisions about the item, such as having kids. You are just making a list of the conversations you want to have.

5. When time is up, do what you did with your *Personal Growth* Mind Map and group things together by theme. As you do this, seeing what you two want to accomplish or do together in life will be exciting.

6. Now, separate some time to have some conversations about items where there may be a bit of a disagreement. Bring your *Positive Growth Mindset* to these conversations.

In the case of conflict:

- Make sure each of you is committed to maintaining a *Positive Growth Mindset* before trying to discuss solutions.

- Gather the facts before letting emotions get in the way. Take 5 minutes for each of you to separately write down the answers to the following questions in your notebook before coming back together.

1. State the conflict in your own words and perspective.

2. Write down a bullet list of positives and negatives of the life change being presented that conflicts with the other person's desires, such as having kids or not.

3. Consider your partner and their needs. How might this conflict be affecting them (positively or negatively)?

4. Write down 1 to 5 ideas for compromise to come to a resolution.

5. After you have written your answers to these questions, compare with your partner what you have written.

6. Write out what you both collectively decide.

Keep this Mind Map ready for filling out the *Current Assessment* tab under *Personal Growth* on your *Five-Year Plan* Worksheet during your *Summit Event*.

Finalizing Your Personal Growth Current State

You did it! Looking at your Mind Map goals categorized by theme and subcategorized by when you want them to happen should evoke feelings of excitement because these things bring you joy in life and you are about to truly make them happen!

It is now time to move to the next mountain in the range to discover the *Current Assessment* there: the *Mountain of Financial Freedom*.

After you pack your bag from your restful stop at the alpine lake on the Mountain of Personal Growth, you set off to conquer the next mountain on your journey. You enter a vibrant aspen forest and notice a deer eating the grass look up at you and pause. You make eye contact as you walk by peacefully. The deer blinks and resumes its meal. You smile in admiration at this gorgeous creature and take a cue from its peaceful, joyful state.

Next Steps Before Moving On

1. At the end of this chapter, open the *Five-Year Plan* worksheet and fill out the information in the *Current Assessment* tab under *Personal Growth* from the items you down-selected in your Mind Map #5.

2. Once this is accomplished, move on to the next chapters. We will assess the current state of your finances, career, and community goals individually until you have a fully documented current state analysis of your life.

3. If you are using the Conquer Your Summit workbook proceed to this same chapter number in the book to fill out the information.

Chapter 7

The Mountain of Financial Freedom

A big part of financial freedom is having your heart and mind free from worry about the what-ifs of life. – Suze Orman

Over the next mile or so, you see fewer trees and more sunlight, and you realize you are headed into a new section of the trail leading up to the Mountain of Financial Freedom. As you make your way up the incline, the trail becomes more and more packed with rock.

Large boulders and some rock climbing lie ahead of you. As you keep on the path, you realize that this mountain is going to be challenging to ascend, and you must climb over some of the rock features to continue if you are to get to the peak.

Mental Tools

Your Deepest Why

A Positive Growth Mindset

Mind-Body-Spirit Exercise

Before we jump in, I will warn you that uncovering stones can be a little scary. Who knows? A spider might jump out at you, or you encounter some nasty gooey slug thing. What I am trying to say is, as you uncover your current state you might discover some uncomfortable things that cause an emotional reaction of some kind. But you, my friend, have the tools; you can recover from whatever might trigger you. Perhaps you feel the sudden weight of debt and you realize you are not set up for a reasonable retirement, or you are just completely lost. It's okay. Deep breath. Remember your *Mind-Body-Spirit exercise*. This will help you reset and start towards your *Positive Growth Mindset* of getting out of these difficult situations.

Everyone starts somewhere, and today is your starting point toward a brighter future. You will understand where you are along your path to *Financial Freedom*, where you want to be, and how you will get there. This chapter will teach you a process for collecting financial information from income to expenses and everything in between.

Before you get started, take a quick moment to review your *deepest why* in your notebook. *Why* are you doing this? *Why* are you ready to make a life plan that will create success for you? Don't be afraid to bring your *Mindset Change Muscle* and turn those negative thoughts into positive mental attitudes.

What Are You Going to Look at in Your Finances?

For this book, it is income and expenses summed up that need to be positive at the end of each month. *Positive* means you have more cash than you spend each month and can therefore look at savings and investments. This is the path toward *Financial Freedom*.

As we continue to peel the finance onion, I want you to understand 2 very fundamental facts about finance:

1. You are putting yourself into **debt** if you spend more than your incoming cash can replenish. Tackle the debt with a dedicated approach to remove the overwhelming feelings it can bring with it.

2. If you have more money coming in than you are spending, you should be **saving**. Savings are to be cherished and put into **investments**. Investments will further help your ratio between income and expenses and feed your retirement.

Income

Everyone has different financial stories, situations, and needs. There are many ways to make an income, and everyone has a different life story. Some are far more complicated than others, but at the end of the day, it's still just numbers.

What is Your Yearly Gross Income?

Take a moment to determine your yearly gross income (your pre-tax income). Maybe it's straightforward because you have a salary position and are paid the same paycheck every few weeks. You may be more aligned with gig work and have 3 jobs or make cash on the side doing odd jobs, so tracking how much income you have is more complicated. Regardless of your situation, you need to get the answers to record in your worksheet.

There are plenty of online tools available to help you manage this task, like connecting your bank accounts to online budgeting apps. You can also open a spreadsheet and start listing out all the income sources you have so you can get to the final pre-tax number.

In your *Gross Income (Yearly)* cell within your *Summit Method* worksheet, record your average yearly income. The worksheet will automatically calculate your monthly income, but if you need to change any values, remove the equation and input manually. You can make notes on where it comes from by removing the current text in the notes cells and adding your own.

Example of income *Current Assessment* from the template (This template is always being updated to provide a more useful experience so this picture could be slightly out of date.)

	Person 1	NOTES (A place for you to type whatever you want as needed)	Person 2
Financials			
Income			
Gross Income (Yearly) Pre-Tax	$60,000.00		$60,000.00
Gross Income (Monthly) Pre-Tax	$5,000.00		$5,000.00

≡   Your Why ▾   Current Assesment ▾   Agenda ▾   Five-Year Plan - Personal Growt ▾   Five-Year Plan - Career ▾   Five-

Expenses

Ah, the love-hate relationship we have with expenses. On the one hand, we hate spending money on things we don't want to, such as maintenance, fees, or bills. On the other hand, we love it when we get to buy things like trips to the Bahamas to soak up the sun.

Some people have plenty of money to do what they need and then extra to do what they want. Those people may still have their sights set on growing to yet another level, or perhaps they are the ones who are thinking they want to retire early and need to start figuring out how to do that.

Some people are the opposite, discovering debt that is piling on without seeing a way out. They are doing financial planning to get themselves out of this situation and are learning to handle their finances better to build towards *Financial Freedom*.

Then there is everyone in between. Everyone's plan must fit their needs.

No matter where you fall on this spectrum, you are not alone.

A Campfire Story About Tenacity

As you already know, in my pursuit to make a difference in my financial journey, I moved into an RV. Going into it, I didn't know how much I depended on basic life amenities. I took for granted that I had them easily in life before the RV. Power, water, heat, internet, and a kitchen, to name a few.

In the first weeks of living, I had to quickly adapt to washing dishes in a specific way that conserved as much water as possible. In addition, I had to track power usage and do things like charge my phone at work so we weren't consuming the limited power generated daily from our one solar panel. Since the space was tiny, cooking activities converted to very simple meals and clean eating focused on reducing waste (it's not like we had a big trash can in the yard to throw things away in either!). There was only propane, so everything had to be cooked with a stove, no microwave! On nights when the temperatures dropped down to the 30s, we had to bundle up and have warm blankets ready to go.

What did I learn from all of this?

Gratitude and the ability to think clearly. These are the things you need to transform yourself and build your future.

I became so grateful for everything I had, my connections with those around me, and my ability to center around a minimalist life. Minimalism allows for the mental clarity you need to ask for what you want in life.

This chapter in my life laid the groundwork for moving the dial on my finances. I was able to get into real estate investing and chart a course for early retirement.

Your Financial Freedom Starts with a Single Step

When it comes to *Financial Freedom*, you will have to look at your situation and figure out what you want to change. Maybe it's canceling 4 out of the 5 streaming services you pay for and just leaving 1. Perhaps it's actually setting up budgets for spending and tracking at the end of the month. Other ideas include:

- Eating out less

- Selling an expensive car with a monthly payment to get a cheaper one for a while

- Getting roommates to split the rent payment

- Minimizing spending on "wants"

- Making gifts instead of buying them

- Simply being creative in how you generate new income (think side hustles)

Are you ready to change your life to get in the direction you want to go?

Let's begin.

Get Lean

Now is the time to practice your *Mindset Change Muscle* and convert expenses into an opportunity to tone up and get lean:

1. Look at your expenses and ask yourself, *"What extra items can I trim on my spending? What beneficial expenses exist, and are there any remaining areas to cut down on?"* List out 5 to 10 ideas in your notebook. Some things will be easy to trim once you find them, while others will be more challenging. You will have to make hard decisions about your lifestyle.

Remember, this is an exercise intended for you to reach your potential. You can only get there if you are willing to work hard.

2. Review your spending and tally up your average monthly expenditures for this part. This will include anything you buy: utilities, rent, subscriptions, payments, etc. This is where online budgeting apps or your online banking will be helpful. These apps will often take all your accounts and automatically do all the analysis for you. It will even categorize things to dive deeper into areas you might want to trim.

You may need to gather data from multiple bank accounts or use other spreadsheets to collect all the data first before having a final average monthly value to put into your *Five-Year Plan* sheet. Once you have determined your average monthly spending over the past year, enter it into the cell labeled *Average Monthly Spending*.

If you are struggling with filling out any of the sheets or would like additional help, reach out at www.ConquerYourSummit.com/coaching

Example of expenses *Current Assessment* from the template:

	Person 1	NOTES (A place for you to type whatever you want as needed)	Person 2
Expenses			
Average Monthly Spending	$4,500.00		$4,500.00

☰ Your Why ▾	Current Assesment ▾	Agenda ▾	Five-Year Plan - Personal Growt ▾	Five-Year Plan - Career ▾	Five- ◀

After pulling together all the data, it was clear that my husband and I were both in a lot of debt. We discovered, through our analysis, that it was an excellent decision to move into the RV and embrace minimalism. Rent took up over 50% of our income, and simply eliminating this expense cut our debt paydown timeline from 3 years to just 1.5 years. We traded our $3000/month apartment for a $250/month RV payment.

We also removed unnecessary subscriptions, and since we knew we had less space, we eliminated frivolous spending on knickknacks and collectible things and made a conscious effort to reduce overall spending. After buying an RV, having our first *Summit Event*, and finishing the move out of the duplex, we ended up parking on the streets near our workplace. (It was pretty scary at first because we were kind of homeless.)

We were ready to make sacrifices in life and do the hard work for potential future gain. We chose to live a minimal lifestyle to save some money from our paychecks and stop living a life of debt:

- We walked to work and showered at local gyms.

- We didn't have internet, so we had to go to libraries or local coffee shops to do computer work.

- There wasn't time for watching movies or relaxing at home anymore. Life was about doing hard work to create a lifestyle that would serve our future.

The cool part about living in the RV, though, was that we spent much more time out and about. Over at friends' places, getting more work done towards our goals, and enjoying nature.

We took a path toward being more mindful of our dreams and actions. There were plenty of struggles along the way, but we needed to make a huge lifestyle change to get to where we wanted to go. We actively used our *Mindset Change Muscle* throughout this experience. The difficult times became the fuel that would power our success with the many lessons they brought. I am not asking you to eliminate everything in your life and do something crazy. I am simply painting a picture of a significant lifestyle change and showing you the benefits of thinking positively about it.

Good Debt and Bad Debt

We have been told throughout time that debt is bad and to stay away from it at all costs. Well, I am here to change your mind a little. There is a degree of acceptable 'good debt'. 'Bad debt' is any debt that doesn't feed towards a more significant, longer investment. Good debts usually take the form of a money-making asset, like a house or rental property. If you have debt that causes you to continue to spend more and never get rid of the original debt, this is the worst kind of debt. This is common with large credit card debt.

Let's take a house mortgage, for example. This is a large piece of
debt, but over time you will pay it off if you stay on schedule, and
your home will build equity to give you more money than you
put into it. That's pretty awesome! What an investment! Making
the wrong choices in the housing market, however, can tank your
finances, so it's important to research and understand what you
are doing when working with a large debt opportunity.

Credit card debt that isn't immediately paid off is bad. You must be conscious of
high rates (unless you pay off the balances regularly). When you pay your credit
cards on time, even if you can't pay the full balance right away, your credit score
will increase. A good credit score will allow you to have more opportunities as
your *Financial Freedom* grows.

Debt can certainly be confusing. Navigating this might make you want to give up,
cry, pull your hair out, and stare blankly at the wall.

Fear not! There are options and various methods to help you manage and
understand the path of improving your debt situation and getting out of it. Do a
quick online search yourself and find what method works for you!

Together, we will analyze your debt so you can start making intelligent,
data-driven decisions to find the correct solutions to fix your life needs. Now, I
want you to look up and record all your debts (your mortgage [real estate debt],
credit card, car loans, personal loans, etc.). Find them all and record the totals
in the *Debt (Bad)* and *Debt (Good)* sections of the *Current Assessment* tab of the
worksheet.

Example of debt *Current Assessment* in the template:

	Person 1	NOTES (A place for you to type whatever you want as needed)	Person 2
Debt (Bad)			
Credit Card Debt	$21,000.00		$21,000.00
Student Loan Debt	$15,000.00		$15,000.00
Car Loan Debt	$7,000.00		$7,000.00
Personal Loan Debt	$2,500.00		$2,500.00
Other Bad Debt	$15,000.00		$15,000.00
Current Bad Debt Total	$60,500.00		$60,500.00
Debt (Good)			
Real Estate Debt	$300,000.00		$300,000.00
Business Debt	$3,000.00		$3,000.00
Other Good Debt (money making assets)	$3,000.00		$3,000.00
Current Debt Total	$306,000.00		$306,000.00

☰   Your Why ▾   Current Assesment ▾   Agenda ▾   Five-Year Plan - Personal Growt ▾   Five-Year Plan - Career ▾   Five-

Savings

 This is the financial topic everyone likes most. Arriving at the savings portion of your plan means you have beat the income and expenses equation to make it into the positive. Yay! But if it's so fantastic and exciting, why don't more people have savings?

Let's be honest, it's just not easy. It takes work to get into the situation of having savings in the first place. Even when you do, the temptation to spend that money on the things you want is very high. Having savings requires discipline and remembering the greater goal.

You need to pick how much you will move into a savings account each month—and track it to make sure you are actually doing it. Once you set that amount, anything above that can go toward whatever you want or you can add more to your savings beyond your standard monthly goal.

To fill out the *Current Assessment* tab for savings, you will need to figure out 3 things:

1. Your *Committed Minimum Bank Account Balance:* This is what you are using as a personal commitment to make sure you never go below this number in your bank account balance. It's your rainy-day minimum and emergency fund.

2. Your *Average Monthly Savings Allocation:* This is what you currently set aside every month for savings. If it's different every month, write down what you do on average. If you don't currently contribute to your

savings, write $0 and make a note in your notebook to focus on this when developing your financial goals in your *Five-Year Plan*.

3. Your *Current Total Savings:* This is where you will add up any cash savings you currently have.

Example of savings *Current Assessment* in the template:

	Person 1	NOTES (A place for you to type whatever you want as needed)	Person 2
Savings			
Commited Minimum Bank Account Balance	$2,000.00		$2,000.00
Average Monthly Savings Allocation	$1,500.00		$1,500.00
Current Total Cash Savings	$10,000.00		$10,000.00

Your Why ▾   Current Assesment ▾   Agenda ▾   Five-Year Plan - Personal Growt ▾   Five-Year Plan - Career ▾   Five- ◂

You must have a savings plan to succeed and achieve your more significant financial goals. These savings will grow until there is enough to transform them into the investments you want to grow so you can reach *Financial Freedom*.

Investments

 Last but not least is investments. (This is my favorite part!) Once you have harnessed the areas of income, expenses, debt, and savings, you are ready to channel their combined powers to support your dream future.

Maybe you aim to retire early to travel, spend time with your family, or buy a fancy car. You can live your dreams with your investments. To do this though, you have to create your plan. Here are some basic starting thoughts for your investment planning:

1. Build up a proper amount of emergency reserve in your bank account.

2. Have a spending budget you will stick to that works for your lifestyle.

3. Keep building up your savings until you have enough to start your first investment. This number will be dependent on what investment strategy you are trying to accomplish. (Buying stocks, buying a house, contributing to a Roth IRA, investing in a business, etc.)

4. Watch your investment grow and make changes in the strategy over time

as needed.

5. Keep saving to get into your next investment.

6. Invest again!

7. Keep following this process of saving and investing until you have enough money to financially support yourself without working.

You are now in *Financial Freedom*! Celebrate your success—but just remember to stay on track! Note that investing isn't the only path to *Financial Freedom*. There are many ways to use your career and side job opportunities to develop other forms of passive income that will feed your *Financial Freedom*. You should explore those ideas in the *Career Success* section of the book.

...Don't be afraid to invest. Get advice from trusted people or sources. You must go out and learn for yourself and decide what is right for you...

The Right Investments for Me

I was thankful to have started my career in a company with a matched 401k where I could build up long-term retirement wealth over time. I also put money into my Roth IRA each year and felt like I was probably set. I had no idea what it would take to retire or how to look at *Financial Freedom* to free myself from a 9 to 5 job.

Ultimately, I decided that I would make much more money in real estate than with a 401k, IRAs, or the stock market, so I went full-bore in that direction.

I had to pay the penalties to unlock my retirement accounts, but I made more returns on my 401K cash through my real estate investment company than I was making in the stock market at that time, so the fees didn't matter in the end.

I spent 10 years making many life mistakes—and celebrating many successes—to get to where I was when writing this book. Everyone's scenario is different, but one thing is for sure: very few people magically get rich overnight. You too can put in the work to achieve where you want to go, regardless of where you currently are.

Learning to Invest Takes Time

Every strategy takes time and education to understand what is happening, regardless of what the get-rich-quick YouTube "gurus" preach online.

Whatever your situation is, your first step in improving it is to (you guessed it!) gather the data so you can record it in the *Summit Method* worksheet. Make sure you have a complete picture of your current investments. If you have ideas for future investments, write them down in your notebook for your *Five-Year Plan* activity.

Example of investments *Current Assessment* from the template:

	Person 1	NOTES (A place for you to type whatever you want as needed)	Person 2
Investments			
401k	$200,000.00		$200,000.00
Retirement Brokerage Accounts (Total) Roth IRA, Traditional IRA	$56,000.00		$56,000.00
Other Retirement Accounts (Total) (Replace this cell with yours)			
Liquid Brokerage Accounts (Total) Stock purchases, bonds, etc	$100,000.00		$100,000.00
Other Investments (Replace this cell with yours)	$0.00		$0.00
Other Investments (Replace this cell with yours)	$0.00		$0.00
Total Opportunity Cash in Investments	$356,000.00	< Update this equation if you created new investment lines	$356,000.00

≡   Your Why ▾   Current Assesment ▾   Agenda ▾   Five-Year Plan - Personal Growt ▾   Five-Year Plan - Career ▾   Five- ◂

Finalizing Your Financial Current State

Use the above pictures and descriptions to help you fill in the numbers in the financial sections of the *Summit Method* worksheet. This is the work that is required to get to the next level. If you have never done this type of work before, don't feel bad or discouraged. Use your *Positive Growth Mindset* to change your excitement level about doing something new that will help your life.

Once you have completed filling in all the numbers, the summary cells will help you see how the data stacks up for your current situation. When you do this, it should be a pretty awesome experience (regardless if it's good or bad). If it makes you feel a bit uneasy, just remember that *Mindset Change Muscle*: Say to yourself, "Wow, learning the facts and details is overwhelming and I'm not sure how to grow or fix my situation...but!... It is good to finally learn this and I am ready to make the moves required to get to where I want to go"

You will unlock your potential and reach *Financial Freedom* if you put in the hard work to do so. It all starts with a plan.

The path you just took required extensive rock climbing, but you see now that as you make your way down to the next mountain's base, the trail is beginning to clear as scattered trees approach. You spot a stream crossing, and you are careful with each step to ensure you pick the right stone to hop to when crossing the water, so you don't fall in. As you focus on your footing, the sounds of nature become center stage. It's peaceful and stimulating, causing you to relax and trust your intuition. The trek becomes smoother since you begin to be able to plan your next step easier.

Next Steps Before Moving On

1. Open the *Current Assessment* tab in your *Summit Method* worksheet. In the financials cells, record all the answers to your current state for income, expenses, debt, savings, and investments. Complete this before moving on to the next chapter. (Example below)

2. If you are using the Conquer Your Summit workbook proceed to this same chapter number in the book to fill out the information.

	Person 1	NOTES (A place for you to type whatever you want as needed)	Person 2
Financials			
Income			
Gross Income (Yearly) Pre-Tax	$60,000.00		$60,000.00
Gross Income (Monthly) Pre-Tax	$5,000.00		$5,000.00
Expenses			
Average Monthly Spending	$4,500.00		$4,500.00
Debt (Bad)			
Credit Card Debt	$21,000.00		$21,000.00
Student Loan Debt	$15,000.00		$15,000.00
Car Loan Debt	$7,000.00		$7,000.00
Personal Loan Debt	$2,500.00		$2,500.00
Other Bad Debt	$15,000.00		$15,000.00

+ ≡   Your Why ▾   Current Assesment ▾   Agenda ▾   Five-Year Plan - Personal Growt ▾   Five-Year Plan - Career ▾   Five- ◂

Chapter 8

The Mountain of Career Success

The only way to do great work is to love what you do. If you haven't found it yet, keep looking. Don't settle – Steve Jobs

The feeling of accomplishment radiates through you and pumps you with energy to find the next peak in your journey. As you look at your map, you see the Mountain of Career Success as the next stop.

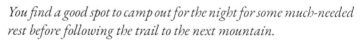

You find a good spot to camp out for the night for some much-needed rest before following the trail to the next mountain.

As you rise to a new day full of new adventures, you find yourself starting to use the Positive Growth Mindset more naturally, and rather than complain about the chill of the morning, you are excited and thankful for clear skies.

Where Do You Want to Be?

Think about where you are and where you want to be in your career.

You might not even honestly know where you want to be right now, but you will soon!

Take the time now on this mountain climb to think about what you do with most of your daily life, which generally means...what you do for work or your career.

What Is Your Current Career?

Maybe you went to college for a full-time position and plan to stay in that industry until you retire. Or perhaps you are a freelance artist working gig to gig in an ever-changing life path. In either scenario or anything in between, you have a career.

Many limit the idea of a career to the big fancy skirt-wearing professionals working in the stuffy office buildings, pouring away at a computer. No. A career is what you spend your time on which, in return, gives you an income, and, as we discovered in the last chapter, income is essential for analyzing wealth. In most cases, you spend more time at your job than doing anything else (except maybe sleeping!).

What Can a Career Mean for You?

You might make a career out of doing 3 different types of jobs at the same time or focus on 1 industry for your entire life. Perhaps you change your field altogether every 5 to 10 years. A job does not have to be lifelong. It's as long as you need it to be to reach *Financial Freedom* or come to an age of retirement where your retirement savings can kick in to help you during old age. Regardless of your situation, your career is essential in your planning because it is, most of the time, a considerable part of your life.

You need to understand where you are in your career today, what it means to you, and how you want to grow. Once your career thoughts are laid out, you can shape your life exactly the way you want it.

I Planned How I Wanted to Grow

I thought I knew exactly what I wanted to do in life and that it would continue that way until I retired. I was fresh out of college with an Aerospace Engineering degree, bright-eyed and bushy-tailed. I was in a spacecraft design engineer starting position, and I set my sights high. I wanted to become a Responsible Engineer for an entire spacecraft design phase and continue from there. These roles would stack up and give me the knowledge and experience needed to get a department manager role. After 3 years, I became a Responsible Engineer for a Japanese geo-communications spacecraft, and I was flying high! I did it!

I am constantly growing and striving because that motivates me in life, and it didn't take long before the question was, *"What can I do now?"*

I knew my leadership skills were growing, and I wanted to get into people and team management. In addition to becoming a Responsible Engineer for several more spacecraft over the next couple of years, I started doing project management on process improvements as a side part of my job at the company. This allowed me to continue what I was doing but also grow my skills.

As I mentioned before, in my industry, it was common for it to take 15 to 20 years to be qualified to become a manager. I had the talent and skills, but time was against me. I wasn't going to let that bring me down, though, and I continued to push and try for the job. After about a year, I was finally selected to take over the 50-person team as a Technical Department Manager. After just 6 years of working there, I had done it! I reached the next milestone of success in my career journey.

I am generally ready to pack my backpack again and start climbing toward my next mountain, but I realized that I wouldn't be able to make a real change and a positive direction for the company I was working for.

I had been on a process improvement project for 3 years, moving way too slowly, and the executives could not make decisions for change and progress. The company was old, had a *Fixed Mindset*, and was unwilling to take the steps toward the change it needed to take off in a better direction into the future of manufacturing. I could not work in a stagnant culture anymore, using all of my precious energy to constantly push for a functional environment.

I was done!

My Next Summit

This was when I set my sights on a startup!

I always loved change, and I figured since I lived in Silicon Valley, I had better try the startup environment of fast-paced fun! Better yet, if I found an aerospace startup that would align with my expertise, it would be so serendipitous!

I researched some in the area and emailed their team. I was contacted by the president of one of them the next day.

After a couple of weeks of odd interviews and pure startup madness that I wasn't used to since I came from the old-school corporate world, I got the job! I would be employee number 7 at a space startup and was excited about what my future might hold! I reached my next summit of working at a start-up. As a woman in aerospace, I was very proud of the hard work and dedication I put in to grow in a field predominantly centered around men.

The Climb Is for Self-Discovery

I had many plans for myself in my career, and when I reached the first goal, I set a new goal. But it wasn't just about going arbitrarily higher and higher. It was about learning who I was and what I wanted to do. I spent time thinking about it. I looked deep into where I wanted to be and what that might look like.

I may have gone to school to become an Aerospace Engineer, but during my first 6 years of working, I realized I had incredible skills in managing people. I loved bringing them together for a project and motivating them to succeed. I also came to find I had excellent project and program management skills and didn't enjoy designing mechanical parts and assemblies that much after all.

And because I had learned who I was and brought that confidence with me when I applied for the Program Manager position at the startup, I got the job!

TOP OF THE MOUNTAIN TIP

...I want you to embrace that it is okay to do a career and completely change your mind at some point. You may be an engineer and realize you want to open a bakery. That is how life works, we are constantly growing, and the most successful people take the time to plan, think, and realize that they might need to change to increase their potential...

It's Okay to Wear Many Hats!

I moved from Engineer to Program Manager, and from there, I became Vice President of Program Management within 6 months of starting at the company. I built the company's business operations in that position from 10 to 150 employees.

In a startup, you wear many hats. Even though I was managing our first spacecraft from the design all the way to its launch into space as a Program Manager, I also became the Head of Business Operations. I was handling purchasing, building up supply chain processes, managing the facilities, creating our IT infrastructure, assisting in finance, supporting as placeholder human resources, aiding in marketing and branding, and performing as executive assistant to the CEO. In doing all these roles, I focused on building the company's culture as a teamwork-based, positive, and respectful workplace.

There were many struggles along the way, and I learned a lot from this experience. I was there for 3.5 years until I realized a new evolution in who I was.

I quit my job in that startup company to take a sabbatical and embrace a new life. During the first couple of months, I freed myself through meditation, positive thinking, and tapping into what life could be. From there, I centered around a small list of my life passions to work toward building a business of my own.

If I could climb to the top of multiple mountains in my engineering career, I knew that I could climb even more mountains if I allowed myself to focus on my talents. I went from living in the streets in an RV to successfully being my own boss and financially free, you too can get to your goals if you put your mind to it and put in the dedication to get there.

Your Turn!

You, too, can change and evolve. You have more control than you think. You also can choose your profession and how you want to grow in it.

Figure out what you want to do by determining how you want to grow. Each time you check in with your plan, make updates that will be critical to finding that future.

When I started making my first *Five-Year Plan* for what my career looked like, none of it pointed to books, art, music, and real estate. My first cut was how I would keep going in that same company and go to different roles for many years. I set a long-term goal of maybe going to a startup one day, but my initial career plan was fuzzy. You will be surprised at how much something can change even just within 3 months, and your whole course will move differently. When the choice comes to moving directions, do it! Alter the plan and keep hiking your Mountains of Success.

Making Money

A career is what you do with most of your daily life. You should strive to find happiness and passion in it, but at the end of the day, you are doing it for an income to feed your financial planning. For any lost person who does not know what to do or how to survive financially independently, focus on learning a trade that will make you money. For someone with a proper safety net and form of financial security, the right choice might be doubling down on your passion and making it valuable.

Find out what you like doing best, and get someone to pay you for doing it. – Katharine Whitehorn

The more value you create, the better your chances are of generating income from your passions. Most of us, however, are not lucky enough to have the financial security to do whatever we want without thinking about how we will pay the bills or live independently. Others may spend a lot of time on their passions without any real knowledge of business or how business works, so they don't know how to turn their passions into viable income streams.

If this is you, I recommend you focus around 70% of your energy on generating income through strategic decisions. Pick lucrative trades so you can start investing as soon as possible.

The remaining 30% can go toward passion projects. This will provide a more balanced income. With the focus on income, you can learn more, track your financial journey, and make the money moves required to become financially free.

Don't quit your day job to follow that passion full-time until you are ready. Focusing on your career and building hobbies on the side is an excellent safe approach at the beginning of your life planning journey. Then you can build your passions up to be your main career if that is something you strive for.

I am not saying you should live a soulless life (obviously factor in time for rest and recreation!). I am saying that focusing hard, in the beginning, to set yourself up for success will allow you to explore and follow your passions freely in the long term.

Career Success Mind Map

Mind Map #6: *What roles, skills, or accomplishments do I want out of my career?*

 It's Mind Map time again! Set a timer for 5 minutes and break out your notebook. I want you to make the center question:

What roles, skills, or accomplishments do I want out of my career?

When you are done, look for themes and see if you can pull anything that needs to be in your plan.

Finalizing your Career Current State

For your career entry data, I want you to record your current employer, title, any relevant skills you want to note, and a short description of what you do there. If at any time you are inspired by an idea for your career growth, feel free to jot it down in your notebook for your first *Summit Event*.

The *Summit Event* is where the magic of creating that *Five-Year Plan* comes together.

You have the power to break through and be who you want to be if you put in the energy and have the drive to get there.

 ...Find a mentor! Mentors in the field you want to grow in can be a valuable asset. They will give you educated feedback so you aren't taking stabs in the dark. Surround yourself with those who live the life you want to live...

Example of career *Current Assessment* from the template:

	Person 1	NOTES (A place for you to type whatever you want as needed)	Person 2	NOTES (A place for you to type whatever you want as needed)
Career Success				
Where do you work?	Company Name: company X Title: Title Y Skills: List out skills		Company Name: company X Title: Title Y Skills: List out skills	
What do you do?	Short Description of what you do: Any other information you want to record down		Short Description of what you do: Any other information you want to record down	

| ≡ | Your Deepest Why ▾ | Current Assesment ▾ | Agenda ▾ | Five-Year Plan - Personal Growth ▾ | Five-Year Plan - Finances | ◄ ► |

The restful sleep and clear skies of the day really set you up for a great day of hiking. The Mountain of Career Success was nothing but endless views of beauty into the valleys and streams below. You could feel life's energy blowing in the breeze. This mountain fueled you with everything you needed to motivate yourself to the next peak to live a fulfilled life.

Next Steps Before Moving On

1. Open the *Current Assessment* tab in your *Summit Method* worksheet. In the *Career Success* cell, record all the answers to where you are today in your career. Complete this before moving on to the next chapter.

2. If you are using the Conquer Your Summit workbook proceed to this same chapter number in the book to fill out the information.

Chapter 9

The Mountain of Community

I alone cannot change the world, but I can cast a stone across the waters to create many ripples. – Mother Teresa

After climbing up 3 different mountains, you have reached the 4th mountain on your map, the Mountain of Community. The journey thus far has been a little lonely as you take this trek by yourself, but when you come to the trailhead of this mountain, you see a few hikers up ahead.

Having not interacted with people in a while, you scurry up to say hi and make some friends on the trail. The mountain is majestic—and truly breathtaking.

You and your new friends decide to take lunch on a fallen tree stump that has a perfect view of the valley below. There you see a soaring eagle returning to its nest perched high up in a tree. You are amazed that even out in a seemingly alone wilderness, you are surrounded by so much life and community in all its forms.

You are absolutely crushing it! Making your way through the current state of your *Mountains of Personal Growth, Financial Freedom, and Career Success.* You're amazing! You now need to plot the ascent to your final *Mountain of Success: Community Impact.*

Humans are best served by interacting with people and learning from others. We are motivated and fueled by how we affect each other. *Community Impact* is built into our nature as people. We developed and evolved with the community around us, so it's unnatural to be isolated in your home, car, and work-life bubbles. Therefore, you need to work on making people a part of your plan in life.

A Campfire Story About Connection

I spent a much-needed mental break to reset from the trials of my corporate life, and I began to mentally become the person I always wanted to be. I had the space and clarity to grow, change, and embrace a new future with a positive outlook. This was hugely stimulating for my mind and soul. I could connect with myself through meditation in ways I had never given myself the time to explore in the past and get out of negative spirals.

While riding the wave of newfound joy and freedom, I realized that this shiny new "perfect" life was beginning to tarnish. The truth of what was missing was becoming more apparent each day. Like a dark cloud approaching to cover the sun, depression seeped its way into my life. I had finally left a career that left my mental health in pieces and built myself back up to being what I thought was everything I ever wanted. I then realized what was missing:

Community

I had left all my friends and family in California to be fully united with my husband in Illinois where his job took him. But while he was at work all day, I was alone. After several months of trying to figure out how to address my loneliness and depression, I gathered that while freeing myself from my previous job was something I desperately needed in my life, I did not understand the value of the *Community Impact* I left behind in the process and how that would affect my ability to belong.

I spent 10 years in the industry and interfaced with 50 to 100 people daily. All-day meetings, break room chats, social hours, and outside events. All these interactions gave me friendship, connectedness, and a sense of purpose. The purpose of belonging.

Without *Community* actively engaged, it didn't matter how many mountains I tried to conquer. I did not have the strength to accomplish anything. I wasn't whole. I have learned how much *Community* transforms my daily existence to continue climbing toward my other mountains. Without goals and execution centered around my *Community* goals, I fall back into these pitfalls of pain.

Record Your Journey: Defining Community for Yourself

Community is a broad term, and every person will define community differently. Family units, tight-knit friend groups, or social connections in line with a certain profession might come to mind.

To best define it for yourself, ask yourself what you want in a community in your life. Grab your notebook, and let's start with a quick exercise. On a new page, write down this question:

What does community mean to me?

Now, spend a few minutes writing down your definition of a *Community* before continuing. As you read this chapter and get new ideas, feel free to add to your definition.

Let's jump into the main categories of focus for *Community*: family, friends, and external societal interactions.

Family

When it comes to family, I work on planning how to engage each year in person and maintain frequent digital communications. Short, quick calls with my immediate family make for much better long-term growth. If you struggle to connect with family members because it feels daunting, try brief communication tactics:

- A simple text saying, *"Hi, How are you doing?"* or *"Hi! Thinking of you. Have a great day!"*

- Start a family group text chat and share about your lives. Post a picture every week or share something happening in your life.

- Call a family member and say *"Hey, there! I am driving to work and I just wanted to say hi and see how you are doing."*

- Start simple with regular weekly texts or group chats.

 As most of us know, family comes in all sorts of shapes, sizes, and complications. Family does not have to be the blood relatives that raised you or didn't raise you your whole life. Family is the people who surround you and support you without question.

I want you to think of family and how you define it for yourself. When I think of family, it's my immediate family on the first shelf. I hate to say there are different shelves for people in life, but without priorities and organization, we would all be lost.

I first focus on how I engage with my immediate family. I want to ensure I am fueling a relationship with each of them and finding ways to serve them in life.

During my *finding your deepest why* exercise, I determined my short list of life purposes that I live for, and one of them is to help and serve others. To do this, I focus every week on how I am trying to better the lives of people around me. Once I know I am covering my bases with the immediate family, I go to the next shelf of extended family members like aunts, uncles, cousins, etc. Regardless of whether they need help, I want to continue to connect and build on our relationships, especially when they are far away. If you struggle to connect or build relationships with people, you must remember one essential thing: *effort*. Whether you like it or not, building a relationship will not just happen magically overnight without you putting in the effort to maintain the connection.

Your Turn!

Try it out today. I want you to scan your phone and find a family member or friend and say, *"Hey there! I was thinking about you, and I hope your day goes awesome!"* You could also send an inspirational quote or a simple *"Hey! How are you doing?"*.

 TOP OF THE MOUNTAIN TIP *...Create a message, copy and paste it to every family member and friend on your phone with whom you wish to connect. This may seem disingenuous, but in reality, it is genuine that you want to reach out to those people. The conversations that flow from that first message are where genuine connections form regardless of whether it was sent as the same original message. Make the time to reach out...*

Focusing on creating communication every other week or each month will create a presence between you and your *Community*. Eventually, they will respond, and the conversations will seem much easier over time. Next thing you know, you will be on the phone having a great call, and there are zero burdens.

What are you waiting for? Pick up your phone and connect with someone now!

Record Your Journey: How Do You Want to Experience Your Family Life?

The fun part about the concept of *Community* is that it's like Play-Doh. You can mold it into whatever you want it to look like with any definition you choose. You just need to actually pick up the dough and start making something. To shape your family life the way you want it, ask yourself the following questions, and feel free to answer in your notebook:

1. *What is my definition of family?*

2. *Do I have different tiers of importance/closeness for people? If so, what are they?*

3. *What are my goals or thoughts surrounding how I want to interact with my family?*

4. *Is there anyone in my family I want to grow my connection with?*

5. *What is one thing I can commit to that will help me better engage with family?*

Find your goals for your family connections and ask yourself what your mindset is toward it. Is it positive and growth-minded? If you feel like your mindset could use some adjustment, flex your *Mindset Change Muscle* and start working out a new method of thinking about family communications.

Time

It can be daunting to catch up with your family because you might think, *"Do I have enough time for a long call right now?"* Most of the time, you won't, and you will put it off, letting it grow into an even more unfeasible task.

For the times when you think to call and you really do have an open schedule, you will also put it off because of the mindset you have labeled the interaction to be: *daunting*. Change your mindset!

If it helps, remember to set boundaries. Sometimes it feels scary, but when you are on the call, just say you have 10 minutes to talk and want to hear how things are going. By setting the call length in the beginning, you have placed a boundary for yourself that you can commit to and feel good about.

Over time by selecting these types of boundaries, you will ease yourself into being excited to jump on a call or meet up with someone. It's your family. They aren't going to punish you because you only had 10 minutes to talk to them. They will continue to love you and appreciate that you have the strength to set what you need and that you gave them some of your time.

Yes, there is only a limited amount of time every day, but if you have a goal, you must update your habits and focus to see that goal through to completion (aka enjoying the benefits of a stronger bond with those around you!). Here are some time-saving hacks for showing love on the go:

- When you are eating your breakfast, make it a habit to send a quick *hello* text message to family members.

- While driving to work, call one family member for a quick check-in.

- Find ways to add reminders to your daily activities, like putting a sticky note on your bathroom mirror that you will see every morning when you brush your teeth saying "Text Aunt Becky!".

- I tend to call up my mom and my sister every couple of days or so, sometimes on a group call, and we all just chat about whatever is happening on that particular day. This regular call, sometimes long, other times concise, makes us each feel more connected to each other.

Once you move past the casual texts and occasional phone calls, it's time to graduate to the next level. Yes, you need to actually physically interact with people. Depending on the situation, this can seem a little scary because people like to be in their shell of control.

...Remember your Positive Growth Mindset. You need to leverage that Mindset Change Muscle, figure out ways to be excited, and set boundaries for yourself at family events...

Try to figure out when you can get as many people together as possible once a year or so. It doesn't always work out, but perfect attendance is not the point. The point is to spend time with those who can make it. Some people have small tight-knit families, while others are huge! You must do what is best for you.

Friends

Sometimes, being with your best friend, is all the therapy you need. – Unknown

Friends are the next pillar of your *Community*.

My friends are everything to me. They are basically family. For my relationships with friends, I spend a lot of effort cultivating and continuing to grow these connections. Your goals might include making new friends, keeping old friends, becoming closer to the ones near you, or cutting out toxic people.

Record Your Journey: Friend Reflection

Take some time to think about your friends today. Reflect on how each of them serves you in life and how you would like to help them in return. In my notebook, I have written a list of everyone in my life who I consider to be my *best* friends.

You might have many acquaintances or people you enjoy being around, but we are talking about real friends here. People you have a connection with. These *best* friends are the ones I have curated a list for; they are the ones with whom I want to keep a solid connection and not lose contact over time. Write your list of current friends down in your notebook and ask yourself the following questions:

1. *What kind of relationship do I have with them?*

2. How often do I want to hang out with and see them?

3. Are they temporary, or do I wish I could keep them forever?

4. In what ways do they serve me? Do I serve them?

Once you have that list of people and have determined their level of importance in your life, focus on the ones you need to strengthen. Maybe some of them don't live near you, so you must create an action plan to visit them with mini goals.

You will need these mini-goals to help you when you fill out your *Five-Year Plan* for *Community* goals. For now, you want to record your current situation with friends and family and write your list and engagement status with those people in the *Current Assessment* tab on your worksheet.

Example of community *Current Assessment* from the template:

	Person 1	NOTES (A place for you to type whatever you want as needed)	Person 2
Community			
Family		I want to KEEP strong relationships with the following people.	
		I want to GROW or create relationships with the following people.	
		List specific CURRENT GOALS for family you currently are working on, not new ones.	
	Keep: Name, Name, Name Grow: Name, Name, Name Current Goals: Goal, Goal, Goal		Keep: Name, Name, Name Grow: Name, Name, Name Current Goals: Goal, Goal, Goal
Friends		I want to KEEP strong relationships with the following people.	
		I want to GROW or create relationships with the following people.	
		List specific CURRENT GOALS for friends you currently are working on, not new ones.	
	Keep: Name, Name, Name Grow: Name, Name, Name Current Goals: Goal, Goal, Goal		Keep: Name, Name, Name Grow: Name, Name, Name Current Goals: Goal, Goal, Goal
External		What external communities are you involved in?	
		Record any CURRENT GOALS you are actively working towards with regards to external community.	
	External Communities: Name, Name, Name Current Goals: Goal, Goal, Goal		External Communities: Name, Name, Name Current Goals: Goal, Goal, Goal
Legacy		Are you working on anything currently that provides towards your legacy?	
	Current Legacy Work: Enter work here		Current Legacy Work: Enter work here

Your Why ▾   Current Assesment ▾   Agenda ▾   Five-Year Plan - Personal Growt ▾   Five-Year Plan - Career ▾   Five- ◂

Removing Toxic Presence in Your Life

Another thing to remember and consider here is those who do not serve you. This can be the hardest thing to realize and even harder to do something about.

If someone in your life breaks down the boundaries you set up for yourself, you might need to take a little extra meditation session to really think deeply about it. Ask yourself the hard questions:

1. *How would I feel if that person suddenly moved away or was no longer my friend?*

2. *What's the worst that could happen if they were no longer in my life?*

Breaking up with a lover is impossibly hard. Breaking up with a friend or even family member is equally no easy task. But just like in a romantic relationship, sometimes you know when you need to make a change. It's healthy to ensure you can do the same things for friendships.

A soul-sucking friend will not match the greater self you are looking to become through this book. It is best to surround yourself with people who believe in you and carry the mentalities of who you want to be.

TOP OF THE MOUNTAIN TIP

...Surround yourself with successful people so you can unlock your greatest potential. Do not carry people that bring you down. You must work on creating boundaries for yourself, holding those boundaries, and surrounding yourself with people who emulate the life you love. You got this!...

External Community

I am a social butterfly. I want to continuously build up the community of people around me. I also want to empower my *Community* to do great things on their own for their success. I also acknowledge that I live in a specific community of people in my surroundings and society. When I am in public, I am working to connect with the people I see in the *Community* I live or travel in.

When I started living in the RV full-time, I realized I wasn't really interested in hanging out at home. When you are on the streets or in campsites, you want to be outside or where there is life.

This experience really showed me the importance of *Community*. I was suddenly more focused on making plans to meet up with friends, visiting my family, and making people a part of my life path.

External community includes people you meet or see regularly at:

- Live shows

- Organized societies or clubs

- Volunteer organizations

- Church

- Out shopping or a community city events

- Functions (perhaps friends of friends, other people's family)

- Work

- Public places

You interact with people all the time whether you realize it or not. This is your external societal community. Over time you might connect with someone through random chance or through someone you know. At that point, they graduate from your external community and get to jump into your inner circles of friends and family. You then get to nurture that relationship and watch it flourish.

How You Present Yourself in Public

Your presence and goals in the community shouldn't just revolve around the people you know. Not to sound like your parent, but to master the *Mountain of Community*, it's also important to think about how you want to be seen by your *Community*—basically how you will act while out in public.

We all have seen that person in the grocery store yelling at the cashier because they are waiting in long lines and being impatient. It makes everyone uncomfortable. That person is yelling at someone who might have zero control over the situation.

How are you acting and reacting in public around your fellow humans?

Do you have patience, give a compliment to a stranger that you like her earrings, smile at people, give a wave, and greet people when you walk into a store?

We spend so much time with our heads down and absorbed in our own bubbles. You don't have to go around and say, *"Free hugs for everyone!"*, but you can bring more light into each day with a *Positive Growth Mindset* toward your general interactions. You will be amazed at what opportunities will flow your way with a simple shift in your energy that radiates as you bounce through your day.

This attitude should also extend to building relationships with coworkers and just genuinely caring about those you interact with regularly throughout your life. Set the intention today to bring a little magic to even the most casual of relationships.

Legacy

Remember that the happiest people are not those getting more, but those giving more. – H. Jackson Brown Jr.

 After learning about family, friends, and social interactions, think about your life in its current state. Ask yourself if you have thoughts about what you want to look back on when you are older or anything you want to build into your legacy. Legacy is your impact here on earth. This is where your *Mountain of Community* connects with your life purpose statement from Chapter 1. Your legacy is how you want to impact those around you while you are here. Legacy is what you want to build for your future and the future of others. Take a few minutes to write down your thoughts about how you want to work on your legacy.

Finalizing Your Community Current State

For this section of your *Summit Method* worksheet, use the notes you took down in your notebook throughout the reflections above to form an understanding of your current state. In the cells for *Community*, write down the names of family and friends you care about deeply and would like to continue having strong relationships with.

Consider your current external societal community and write anything about your current state worth noting or community organizations you are currently involved with. If you are currently doing something that feeds towards your legacy, make sure to write that in too. Remember, this is just to record what you are doing right now in life for community goals and execution. You will now explore how to project these goals into your *Five-Year Plan*!

Next Steps Before Moving On

1. Open the *Current Assessment* tab in your *Summit Method* worksheet. In the *Community* cells, record the names of your current important relationships. Add in any *Community* groups you are involved with now or things you are currently doing for your legacy outreach. Complete this before moving on to the next chapter.

2. If you are using the Conquer Your Summit workbook proceed to this same chapter number in the book to fill out the information.

Part Three Summary

You have successfully surveyed your *4 Mountains of Success: Personal Growth, Financial Freedom, Career Success, and Community Impact.* In Part Three, you learned how to document where you stand within these subjects and set yourself up for where you want to go.

In Part Four, you will expand on how to truly master each mountain to climb it quicker, smoother, and more skillfully the next time around. Now, let's go make those goals real!

THE VIEW OF YOUR MOUNTAINS OF SUCCESS

Part Four

Set Yourself Up for the Climb

You decide to set up your own mini Base Camp in a great spot for some much-needed rest from the strenuous initial climbs. You have set up a tent for you to sleep in, have an area for cooking your meals, and are working on how you want to repack your bag for the final leg of the journey: conquering all 4 summits. You decide at this moment to complete each climb better, faster, more efficiently, and with unwavering mental fortitude.

You are not alone here as several other hikers are doing the same thing: preparing for their ascent. You have made a connection with them, and you are excited that for your second climb of each mountain, you won't be alone since you have a community of others to go up with you and support you.

One by one, here you will pack your Five-Year Plan, Two-Year Action Plan, and Quarterly Check-Ins as the next 3 tools in your backpack.

For every mountain you choose to climb in life, the time and energy you put into preparation will determine how smooth the trek will be. Can you imagine heading out on a travel adventure without first aid? If you properly plan for a trip, you will be equipped to face any challenges you might encounter along the way.

This next mountain climb will expand on your current state. It will show you exactly how to create your detailed life plan for the next 5 years within each *Mountain of Success*, which is the first step to making your best life a reality!

Chapter 10

Prioritize Your Personal Growth

Setting goals is the first step in turning the invisible into the visible. – Tony Robbins

This chapter is all about conquering your *Mountain of Personal Growth*. Let's get right into how to meet your *Personal Growth* goals for the next 5 years of your life plan!

Completing Your Brainstorm for Personal Growth Goals

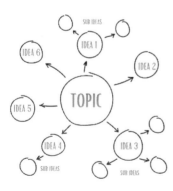

Start by reviewing what you wrote in your current state assessment for your *Personal Growth* or fill it out if you didn't do it after the previous chapters.

Then grab your notebook to review the Mind Map you created in Chapter 6. *(Mind Map #5: What do I want my Personal Growth throughout life to look like?)*

As you have continued through the book since that mind map, more and more thoughts about your life and where you want to go have probably snuck into your brain. Review your original Mind Map and give yourself 5 minutes to add any new ideas.

Once you are done, finish bundling them into themes as applicable. You are figuring out how to prioritize by picking some of the most important of these and planning to do them.

Filling Out the Worksheet

In your *Summit Method* worksheet, you will write in the bullets for years 1 through 5 based on what you plan to accomplish. Years 1 and 2 are shown below from the *Summit Method* worksheet as an example.

Personal Growth Five-Year-Plan				
Starting Month: ENTER HERE	Year/Age	Year 1 Goals	Year/Age	Year 2 Goals
NOTES	2023	Person 1	2024	Person 1
	33	**Hobbies:** Goal, Goal, Goal **Health & Fitness:** Goal, Goal, Goal **Travel:** Goal, Goal, Goal **Big Events:** Goal, Goal, Goal **Education:** Goal, Goal, Goal **Volunteer Work:** Goal, Goal, Goal **Spritual/Meditation:** Goal, Goal, Goal **Other:** Goal, Goal, Goal	34	**Hobbies:** Goal, Goal, Goal **Health & Fitness:** Goal, Goal, Goal **Travel:** Goal, Goal, Goal **Big Events:** Goal, Goal, Goal **Education:** Goal, Goal, Goal **Volunteer Work:** Goal, Goal, Goal **Spritual/Meditation:** Goal, Goal, Goal **Other:** Goal, Goal, Goal
List out your goals for Hobbies, Health & Fitness, Travel, Big Events, Education, Volunteer Work, Spiritual/Meditation, Other Personal Goals for the next five years	2023	Person 2	2024	Person 2
	32	**Hobbies:** Goal, Goal, Goal **Health & Fitness:** Goal, Goal, Goal **Travel:** Goal, Goal, Goal **Big Events:** Goal, Goal, Goal **Education:** Goal, Goal, Goal **Volunteer Work:** Goal, Goal, Goal **Spritual/Meditation:** Goal, Goal, Goal **Other:** Goal, Goal, Goal	33	**Hobbies:** Goal, Goal, Goal **Health & Fitness:** Goal, Goal, Goal **Travel:** Goal, Goal, Goal **Big Events:** Goal, Goal, Goal **Education:** Goal, Goal, Goal **Volunteer Work:** Goal, Goal, Goal **Spritual/Meditation:** Goal, Goal, Goal **Other:** Goal, Goal, Goal

+ ☰   Your Why ▾   Current Assesment ▾   Agenda ▾   Five-Year Plan - Personal Growt ▾   Five-Year Plan - Caree

TOP OF THE MOUNTAIN TIP

...Keep your goals at 3 to 5 per area of success! 3 goals are low enough of a number to be manageable but challenging, and anything over 5 goals could be too overwhelming and puts you at risk of going for 0 goals!...

Victory Sure Is Delicious!

Are you overwhelmed by the thought of carrying out even just one long-term goal over 5 years?

Well, just think of each long-term goal as a big, juicy sandwich.

Every *Five-Year Plan* you create is exactly that, a sandwich:

- The **bottom bread** is the current state of where you are today along that *Five-Year Plan*.

- The **top bread** is the big goal or dream you are striving for in your *Five-Year Plan*.

- The **middle ingredients** are made up of the steps or mini goals it takes to complete the main goal.

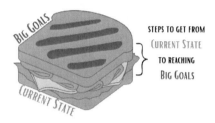

STEPS TO GET FROM
CURRENT STATE
TO REACHING
BIG GOALS

Once you've "made" your planning sandwich, go ahead and take a huge bite out of it! This means taking action and actually **doing** the steps from bread to bread in real life! Don't worry, breaking down each step or mini-goal for the year is easy with *Quarterly Check-Ins*!

Bottom bread: Now, let's apply this concept to the physical data you have collected in your notebook about your *Personal Growth* goals. Your assessment of your current state for each area of success, which should already be complete, is the foundation of the sandwich and where you will start from.

Top bread: Your big goal makes up the top bread. Using your Mind Maps and anything you noted for yourself in your notebook, collect anything that answers the following question:

What are the biggest Personal Growth goals I am focused on completing within 5 years?

Write down your selected biggest *Personal Growth* goals in your notebook or directly into the worksheet if you are ready for that.

Sandwich ingredients: You now need all the exciting and delicious ingredients between your bread slices to fill up years 1 through 5 of your *Five-Year Plan*. For each big goal, create a 1 to 5-step mini plan to accomplish that goal from your now state to the completion state.

Trying to plan out a long-term goal can be overwhelming. With this simplified approach you can get there with ease. Repeat this process with each of your *Mountains of Success* and get started on your biggest goals in life today—one ingredient at a time!

...It's okay if you're having trouble filling in step-by-step details for potentially ambiguous big goals. Sometimes you just don't know what the future will hold, but you can do a quick online search or ask AI what would the standard steps be to accomplish that goal for other people. There is also lots of information on YouTube given our "How To" culture. Do some research and figure out which mini steps make sense for you to accomplish that big goal. The details will naturally fall into place as you learn and become inspired...

Stay SMART

In previous chapters, we talked about **SMART** goals. Make sure you leverage that methodology here when you write out your big *Five-Year Plan* goals.

Saying that you want to lose weight this year as a *Personal Growth* goal isn't good enough. I want you to think harder and **SMART.**

By _____ time, I want to _____ by doing _____.

Specific – **M**easurable – **A**ttainable – **R**ealistic – **T**imebound

By <u>November,</u> **I want to** <u>lose 10 pounds</u> **by** <u>joining my local CrossFit club and eating more healthily</u>**.**

Try putting a specific metric onto the goal and a timeframe within the year you want to achieve it. You don't need to know the exact month or day you will finish, although the more precise you are the better. At a bare minimum, you should at least be able to pinpoint which quarter of the year you want to achieve it in (Q1:January-March, Q2:April-June, Q3:July-September, or Q4:October-December.). This will come in handy during your *Quarterly Check-Ins.*

Some Common Examples to Consider in Your *Personal Growth* Goals:

- *Living situation* – Maybe you have always wanted to move to the big city to try it out for a while. Great! Put it in your plan for a year when it might make sense.

- *Travel* – International vacations, hiking, outdoor trips, visiting friends & family.

- *Education*- Maybe you want to go back to school, learn a new personal trade, or excel in a new skill for your current work. Maybe you want to change careers entirely and work towards making that shift.

- *Milestones & Event Planning* – Getting married, special birthdays, family events, etc.

- *Fitness* – Getting to a certain weight, getting to a specific lifting strength, joining competitions, connecting with your mental health, working on body positivity, flexibility, eating healthy, or cutting out bad habits.

- *Spiritual* – Determining ways to connect to your beliefs differently.

- *Meditation & Mental Health* – Practices you want to learn or grow into.

- *Passion Projects* – These things bring you joy but maybe are just for fun and don't pay the bills for you, also known as hobbies. Working on your music, finishing art pieces, film projects, building up cars, house projects, gifts for people, training programs, learning to sail, etc.

You can choose what you want in life and make it happen

To complete the *Summit Method* worksheet for *Personal Growth*, type out the goals you want to achieve over the next 5 years. Sometimes a goal is for 1 year, and you want to just repeat doing that thing or grow in it over several years until it's a part of your standard life. You don't have to work towards a new thing every year. You can mention that your goal is to continue to retain or grow that 1 goal over time.

Make sure you chart out all your big *Personal Growth* goals over the 5 years in the spreadsheet AND add the necessary 1 to 5 steps to achieve each one across the 5-year timeframe.

Example below from the Summit Method worksheet:

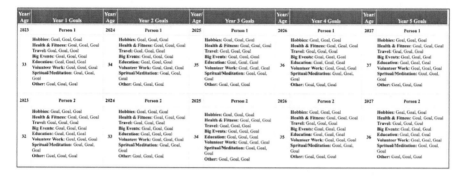

Year/Age	Year 1 Goals	Year/Age	Year 2 Goals	Year/Age	Year 3 Goals	Year/Age	Year 4 Goals	Year/Age	Year 5 Goals
2023	Person 1	2024	Person 1	2025	Person 1	2026	Person 1	2027	Person 1
33	Hobbies: Goal, Goal, Goal Health & Fitness: Goal, Goal, Goal Travel: Goal, Goal, Goal Big Events: Goal, Goal, Goal Education: Goal, Goal, Goal Volunteer Work: Goal, Goal, Goal Spritual/Meditation: Goal, Goal, Goal Other: Goal, Goal, Goal	34	Hobbies: Goal, Goal, Goal Health & Fitness: Goal, Goal, Goal Travel: Goal, Goal, Goal Big Events: Goal, Goal, Goal Education: Goal, Goal, Goal Volunteer Work: Goal, Goal, Goal Spritual/Meditation: Goal, Goal, Goal Other: Goal, Goal, Goal	35	Hobbies: Goal, Goal, Goal Health & Fitness: Goal, Goal, Goal Travel: Goal, Goal, Goal Big Events: Goal, Goal, Goal Education: Goal, Goal, Goal Volunteer Work: Goal, Goal, Goal Spritual/Meditation: Goal, Goal, Goal Other: Goal, Goal, Goal	36	Hobbies: Goal, Goal, Goal Health & Fitness: Goal, Goal, Goal Travel: Goal, Goal, Goal Big Events: Goal, Goal, Goal Education: Goal, Goal, Goal Volunteer Work: Goal, Goal, Goal Spritual/Meditation: Goal, Goal, Goal Other: Goal, Goal, Goal	37	Hobbies: Goal, Goal, Goal Health & Fitness: Goal, Goal, Goal Travel: Goal, Goal, Goal Big Events: Goal, Goal, Goal Education: Goal, Goal, Goal Volunteer Work: Goal, Goal, Goal Spritual/Meditation: Goal, Goal, Goal Other: Goal, Goal, Goal
2023	Person 2	2024	Person 2	2025	Person 2	2026	Person 2	2027	Person 2
32	Hobbies: Goal, Goal, Goal Health & Fitness: Goal, Goal, Goal Travel: Goal, Goal, Goal Big Events: Goal, Goal, Goal Education: Goal, Goal, Goal Volunteer Work: Goal, Goal, Goal Spritual/Meditation: Goal, Goal, Goal Other: Goal, Goal, Goal	33	Hobbies: Goal, Goal, Goal Health & Fitness: Goal, Goal, Goal Travel: Goal, Goal, Goal Big Events: Goal, Goal, Goal Education: Goal, Goal, Goal Volunteer Work: Goal, Goal, Goal Spritual/Meditation: Goal, Goal, Goal Other: Goal, Goal, Goal	34	Hobbies: Goal, Goal, Goal Health & Fitness: Goal, Goal, Goal Travel: Goal, Goal, Goal Big Events: Goal, Goal, Goal Education: Goal, Goal, Goal Volunteer Work: Goal, Goal, Goal Spritual/Meditation: Goal, Goal, Goal Other: Goal, Goal, Goal	35	Hobbies: Goal, Goal, Goal Health & Fitness: Goal, Goal, Goal Travel: Goal, Goal, Goal Big Events: Goal, Goal, Goal Education: Goal, Goal, Goal Volunteer Work: Goal, Goal, Goal Spritual/Meditation: Goal, Goal, Goal Other: Goal, Goal, Goal	36	Hobbies: Goal, Goal, Goal Health & Fitness: Goal, Goal, Goal Travel: Goal, Goal, Goal Big Events: Goal, Goal, Goal Education: Goal, Goal, Goal Volunteer Work: Goal, Goal, Goal Spritual/Meditation: Goal, Goal, Goal Other: Goal, Goal, Goal

Next Steps Before Moving On

1. You don't need to fill out the *Summit Method* worksheet yet, you will do that when you actually do your *Summit Event*. For now, go through the *4 Mountain of Success* Chapters 10-13 to learn how to do the planning techniques. Take any notes in your notebook from this chapter that you want to remember or use when you schedule your *Summit Event*.

2. If you are using the Conquer Your Summit workbook proceed to this same chapter number in the book to fill out the information.

Chapter 11
Financials Without Fail

The most difficult thing is the decision to act – the rest is merely tenacity. – Amelia Earhart

This chapter is all about conquering your *Mountain of Financial Freedom*. Let's get right into how to meet your *Financial Freedom* goals for the next 5 years!

Financial Projection

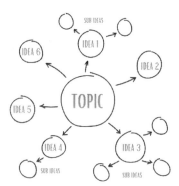

To make it easier to come up with a *Five-Year Plan* for your finances, you will follow this activity. Please gather:

1. Any notes you wrote down when analyzing where you were along your *Financial Freedom* journey from previous chapters.

2. Your current state worksheet in which you recorded your current financial situation.

3. Blank pages in your notebook.

It's Mind Map time!

Mind Map #7: *What does my ideal financial situation look like?*

Set a timer for 5 minutes and start thinking about the future when it comes to income and expenses, aka finances!

Write out all the ideas you have about what financial success would look like to you on that paper. Think about income, expenses, debt, savings, and investments. Remember, there are no bad ideas; just throw everything that comes to mind on the paper.

Ask yourself the following questions to fuel your brainstorming:

Where would you like to be by the end of this year?

Where would you like to be in 5 years?

What's the ideal lifestyle you would like to live in general, and by when do you want to live it?

When you finish the Mind Map, you will have many ideas to help you fill out the boxes on the *Summit Method* worksheet. In the *Overall Goals* cell for each year (example below), I want you to write out a simple, concise statement of what you want to accomplish in that year from a financial standpoint. Do this for each of the 5 years.

Remember to make your *Five-Year Plan* sandwich if you get stuck!

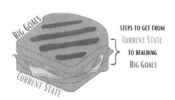

Pick 1 long-term goal (top sandwich bread) and put it in the *Year 5 Goal* cell. Then figure out the mini-step plan to get there (that's the ingredients inside the sandwich) and put them in Years 1, 2, 3, and 4. Fill in your current state (bottom bread). Then, set up *Quarterly Check-Ins* for each year's goal and follow through! *Quarterly Check-Ins* will be discussed in more detail later but it's basically taking those yearly mini-steps and breaking them down a little bit more to what are you going to accomplish each quarter of the year to get to that year's mini-step.

Example below from the Summit Method worksheet:

Financials						
	Current	Year 1 Goal	Year 2 Goal	Year 3 Goal	Year 4 Goal	Year 5 Goal
Overall Goals						

Now we will move into the actual number projection for each financial category. The worksheet will auto-calculate some of the lines for you based on standard practices. If you want to change your numbers, go for it. You should be able to roughly get a feel of what numbers you want your goals to be. To do that, just click on the cell and type whatever you want to write over the original equation.

If any of your *Five-Year Plan* inputs are overwhelming and you think you want to explore other help outside of the book, consider visiting the following site www.ConquerYourSummit.com/coaching.

Income

 Income should be inputted as the yearly gross income before taxes. You need to calculate this for either a salary or an hourly position. I want you first to form a reasonable goal for where you might want to be during Year 1. Depending on when you start this event in the calendar year, you may have a lot or a little time left in that year. Keep this in mind when making your decision as to what to write down. It is also completely okay to keep the same number you are at today through your Year 1. Only you are going to know what is possible and a reasonable goal.

This being said, don't be afraid to push yourself!

How do you do that? There are many ways to start being proactive about what you want in life, and during your *Summit Event*, you are setting goals and expectations to start doing just that. Be bold and take control of your life. Talk with your manager in an open and honest conversation about where you are looking to grow with your job that year. Take your life into your own hands.

Here are some scenarios for income goal ideas in the cells for the next 5 years:

Scenario #1: Perhaps you suspect you might get a raise this year; in this case, you would go to your Year 1 cell and take your current state income number plus whatever you think the raise will be. Then, *stop wishing and go get it*! To show the projection from that raise going forward, take what you would get in an average yearly increase in your wages and make Years 2, 3, 4, and 5 increase by that much for the remaining cells past Year 1.

For example: If your current gross yearly income is $50,000, and you generally get a 3% increase each year, you would write $50,000 in Year 1 and $51,500 in Year 2. Then keep taking 3% of that year's projected income and add that to the following year, making it $53,045 for Year 3, $54,636 for Year 4, and $56,275 for Year 5.

Everyone's situation is different, so you must manipulate the worksheet cells for what works for you for the correct projection. You will then see where you could be in 5 years if you stayed at that same position with your standard increase of maybe 3%. If you don't like the number you see, now is the time for you to start augmenting and changing your plan. Don't be stagnant in your career when it comes to raises or wage increases. If you're stagnant in your yearly raises, you need to be looking to grow. It's also not uncommon to get 10% or more during a job change, and well-planned career moves can net bigger pay raises than just a yearly increase.

Scenario #2: Maybe you plan to quit your job and go to a new place so you can negotiate higher pay. Excellent! Decide which year it makes sense to do something like that and what you want that income bump to be at the new job. Let's say you choose Year 3, so you enter the new salary number desired into that cell. Then, take a standard yearly increase from that new wage and project that forward each year until you get to Year 5 (like the 3% increase in the previous example). Continue to review and adjust the numbers until the plan looks like what you actually want your life to become. It's okay to set your goals high even if you don't know how to achieve them. You want to know your desires first so you can go out and find ways to make them happen.

Scenario #3: For hourly positions, you will need to calculate roughly what a year's worth of wages would be. To do this, you just need to take your hourly wage times your average hours per week and multiply it by 52 for the number of weeks in a year. (**Note:** If you know you take a certain number of weeks or days off in a year, make sure to account for that by subtracting that number from 52.) The income amount is meant to be the gross estimate total before any taxes. Now input in if you have any wage increases planned or project out what you want your wage increases to be over time. This can help you look at time over five years and determine how you want to grow your career to meet those goals.

If trying to calculate pre-tax has you stumped, don't sweat it. Everyone's income situation is different and the template only requires you to input your income in the best way that works for you.

If you are doing this with a partner, I highly suggest you build your plan together so you can see your combined power as a couple. Depending on where you are in your relationship, this could make a lot of sense and catapult you to the next level. There is still value in even newer relationships going through the five-year planning exercise because it will allow you to have some conversations that might not have happened otherwise. It can help the 2 of you grow in a similar direction and learn to support each other. The worksheet has space for you both to input your plans together since Google Sheets allows for simultaneous editing. If you don't want to be showing your partner that information for whatever reason, you can just each have your own file to fill out.

During your *Summit Events* throughout the year, you should always be sharing with each other. Ideally, you should make sure you each have access to the file so you can see each other's plan, support each other, and be able to check in on it from time to time to make sure you can work as a team. Remember when you are doing this with a partner, they are your accountability. You need to push each other to success. Use the *Mind-Body-Spirit exercise* to reset if any of these conversations lead to difficult places. Remember that you are looking to grow and change your life, so carry a *Positive Growth Mindset* and be open to developing into a stronger, more mature person.

You should now use the worksheet and project your income. You can always return to any data entry as you continue this process. It will be iterative as you learn new things and you will have deeper conversations. Like Tetris, we are gathering all the blocks, but we will need to do this one at a time to figure out if we can piece it all together for the best fit.

Example below from the Summit Method worksheet:

Financials	Current	Year 1 Goal	Year 2 Goal	Year 3 Goal	Year 4 Goal	Year 5 Goal
Income						
Gross Income (Yearly) Pre-Tax	$60,000.00	$61,800.00	$63,654.00	$65,563.62	$67,530.53	$69,556.44
Gross Income (Monthly) Pre-Tax	$5,000.00	$5,150.00	$5,304.50	$5,463.64	$5,627.54	$5,796.37

Expenses

It is essential to be able to understand your monthly expenses and track them over time. Many people only have a rough idea of their expenses, but they aren't regularly reviewing the data to really understand the trends. Expenses are everything that leaves your bank accounts—subscriptions, shopping, bills, utilities, loan payments, house payments, etc. You should know your rough average spending per month since the key to not getting into debt is to make sure you are not overspending based on your income.

The mind is a powerful place, and it can easily tell you that everything is fine with its illusions. You must follow a data-driven approach when it comes to expenses and have disciplined execution. This means that on the first of every month, you should be opening all your financial accounts and review your transactions to make sure they are correct. You should be recording them into a categorizable database which you can make yourself or google financial tracking apps or software. This will help you analyze the trends in your spending.

Regularly ask yourself:

Am I within my budget?

Do I need to make any active changes in my lifestyle for the following month to stay on target or get back in line?

Without a diligent approach to how you review, correct, and track your expenses, you will have a poor financial outlook. If you are already tracking your finances, great! If not, you need to start tracking today! If you don't have a way to track monthly finances, Conquer Your Summit provides a basic starter for easy use. Head to www.ConquerYourSummit.com/monthlyfinances to grab it. Start this now, and you will be able to calculate your average monthly expenses to compare to your income. You will need this to fill in your *Average Monthly Spending* into the *Summit Method* worksheet.

In your *Summit Method* worksheet, fill in the five-year projection with what you believe is a reasonable goal for you to spend during Year 1. Then decide if you are looking to decrease, increase or stay the same on spending. In the example below this person is trying to work towards decreasing at a small but steady rate per year to hopefully work towards increasing savings.

The example below is from the Summit Method worksheet:

Financials						
	Current	Year 1 Goal	Year 2 Goal	Year 3 Goal	Year 4 Goal	Year 5 Goal
Expenses						
Average Monthly Spending	$4,500.00	$4,500.00	$4,000.00	$4,000.00	$3,500.00	$3,500.00

Debt

Debt is as important to manage as income, if not more important. There are many types of debt structures, and each has its own unique way of hindering or facilitating your growth.

With bad debts, you quickly see your hard-earned money depleted as you pay fees and interest to maintain it, like consumer credit cards, retail chain cards, and loans for liabilities like cars, vacations, or travel.

On the other hand, some debts actually pay you, and you can see your cash flow increase every month, like real estate loans, business loans, capital equipment like a fleet of rental cars, or equipment to make goods like commercial ovens. These are the good debts!

A Method of Looking at Debts

In this area of the worksheet, you will look at all your debts and write them out. Debts are monthly obligations you must pay, but they are not the same as expenses. Utilities and memberships are examples of monthly expenses, but credit cards, loans, and borrowed monies with interest tacked onto them are bad debts. If you are struggling with debt, I highly suggest searching the internet for options as there are many schools of thought and methods to try to reducing debt. This book isn't meant to teach you all the ways to look at solving debt issues as there are so many fantastic experts on this out there already. One thing you can start with is to organize your debt in a spreadsheet and list out all your debts by name, balance, interest rate, and monthly minimum payment. Then, you make a plan to pay them off, some people start with the smallest balance, pay that off completely as fast as possible by even paying more than the monthly requirement, and then work their way to the higher balances. Other people focus on paying off the balance of the highest interest rate first.

While you are focusing on aggressively paying down your selected account, you will pay the minimum balance on everything else. Repeat that logic all the way down your list until you have no more debt.

Start Chipping Away Now

Once you pick the account you are going to start aggressively paying down first, while other debts remain at the minimum payment, there are some other calculations to help you.

1. Gather all your debt amounts into a spreadsheet.

2. Calculate how long it will take you to pay each of them based on your minimum payments.

3. For the debt item you plan to aggressively target and pay down quickly try different calculation scenarios to see how to figure out your course of action and what speed of payment you can afford based on your monthly income versus expenses. You can adjust your plan with any of the following ideas too. What does it look like:

   a. If you paid the minimum payment.

   b. If you paid 15% of your monthly income to that debt.

   c. If you paid 50% of your income to that debt.

4. Once you pay off the first debt, move to the next one and follow step 3.

How long until you break free?

Evaluating Debt

It's worth noting a few other things about debt. There are 2 sides you can manipulate when paying down debt. You can reduce spending habits to allocate more money to pay debts off or increase income.

The reason we focus so much on debts is that the habit of getting into bad debts will generally keep you broke. Many people, believe it or not, have never been told these aspects of financial education, which is why I am taking a moment to refresh everyone on how to evaluate and break down debt.

The simplest way to judge whether the debt is good or bad is to ask yourself two simple questions:

*Does the debt **put** money in my pocket regularly?*

*or **take** money out repeatedly?*

For many people, the concept of debt putting money into your pocket is so foreign that they can't imagine what that looks like.

Good Debt Is...Well, Good!

The cleanest, easiest example of good debt is real estate:

If you take a mortgage out on a $125,000 home over thirty years, and this debt costs you approximately $900 a month in mortgage, but if you rent it out for $1400 a month, your rent now covers the debt plus puts money in your pocket in the form of cash flow.

Other great examples of good debt include:

- Taking small loans to buy a car to rent out on apps like Turo to make money.

- Investing in a vending machine to create income.

- Investing or buying a turnkey business.

- Investing in the stock market.

Every investment comes with its risks, but in the long run, these debts can put thousands of dollars into your pocket, whereas bad consumer debt will always take from you.

Many people also know very well about bad and good debts, but they struggle with the overwhelming realities in life, which pile up often leading to more and more bad debt. These situations can be very challenging to deal with. I advise you to use your *Positive Growth Mindset*, incorporate the debt strategies, and consider changing your job or position to be able to increase income or create a side business to augment your monthly cash.

Back to the Worksheet!

I want you to review what you filled out for the current state of your debt. Then fill out the monthly payment amount into the equations within the columns for Years 1–5. If a certain type of debt on the list does not apply to you, you can delete all the numbers. The worksheet will sum up your debts and provide you with totals for good and bad debts. Remember to fill these cells out as accurately as you possibly can!

With the debt calculator you made, you should be able to see over time what the decrease in your bad debt will be and project over your *Five-Year Plan* as to when you will be out of that debt.

For your good debt assets, you need to project how those will be going down over time based on the monthly payments that your asset takes care of.

Based on your financial dreams and mind-mapping activities throughout the book, this is also where you will add in more of that good debt over the 5 years if you know you are looking to get into things like buying a house, starting or acquiring a business, or other debt-related investments. Feel free to estimate what the debt might be and input that number in the worksheet on the correct year for you.

If it's too complicated to think about projecting potential new good debt, just write in the cell the written goal you have for yourself in Years 1-5 for establishing these new good debt investments.

The example below is from the Summit Method worksheet:

Financials	Current	Year 1 Goal	Year 2 Goal	Year 3 Goal	Year 4 Goal	Year 5 Goal
Debt (Bad)						
Credit Card Debt	$21,000.00	$15,000.00	$5,000.00	$0.00	$0.00	$0.00
Student Loan Debt	$15,000.00	$10,800.00	$6,600.00	$2,400.00	$0.00	$0.00
Car Loan Debt	$7,000.00	$5,200.00	$3,400.00	$1,600.00	$0.00	$0.00
Personal Loan Debt	$2,500.00	$1,600.00	$700.00	$0.00	$0.00	$0.00
Other Bad Debt	$15,000.00	$13,200.00	$11,400.00	$9,600.00	$7,800.00	$6,000.00
Current Bad Debt Total	$60,500.00	$45,800.00	$27,100.00	$13,600.00	$7,800.00	$6,000.00
Debt (Good)						
Real Estate Debt	$300,000.00	$270,000.00	$240,000.00	$210,000.00	$180,000.00	$150,000.00
Business Debt	$50,000.00	$46,400.00	$42,800.00	$39,200.00	$35,600.00	$32,000.00

Savings

Savings is the money you have extra to store away and use when it is needed. You can calculate this by taking your total yearly income and subtracting your total yearly expenses. This would be how much you saved in that year. Ideally, you want to have a separate savings account that you make a plan to regularly transfer funds into until it is an amount that can be reinvested into money-making investments.

Do You Save or Pay Debt—or Both?

Savings should come after bad debts are paid off. Having savings while also carrying bad debt means you're actually not saving since your debt is still charging you interest, so it makes sense to pay off your debts first. You will get faster growth once released from the burdens of bad debt.

If you have absolutely zero dollars and can't pay your monthly bills or rent, then paying debt and having savings is off the table. You need to increase your income by exploring new ways to change your career track.

Your Committed Bank Account Minimum

If, let's say, you are in the camp of under $1000 in your bank account monthly, then my suggestion is to save until you get to that $2000 minimum balance mark and strive to keep that buffer going forward as you start paying down debts. For some families at higher risk of fluctuations, it might make more sense to save a larger buffer, say $1000 per family member, as opposed to the flat $2000 amount from above, and then start paying off debt. Your buffer is your *Committed Bank Account Minimum* in the *Summit Method* worksheet.

Average Monthly Savings Allocation

Let's talk saving strategies! Simply choose one of the following saving rules—the one that suits you best:

50/30/20

Spending Profile:

- 50% – Essentials

- 30% – Wants

- 20% – Savings/debts

80/20 – *This person doesn't want to figure out how to separate essentials from wants*

Spending Profile:

- 80% – Life Expenses

- 20% – Savings/debts

85/15 or 90/10 – *This person doesn't need the larger savings*

Spending Profile:

- 85-90% – Life Expenses

- 10-15% – Savings/debts

Basically, income minus expenses minus debt payments will equal your rough savings left over.

To fill out the cells for the *Average Monthly Savings Allocation* section of the *Summit Method* worksheet, you need to review what you put in for your current state. Then you will look at what you have for income, expenses, and debt already inputted into your plan. You should now be able to take that data and project over the 5 years what kind of savings that will give you.

As you input the numbers, you can determine if you like the look of what kind of savings you would be getting yearly and over the five-year time frame. If you don't like what you see, now is the time to keep iterating through the plan on what you are doing to change your situation to make it more in line with where you want to be in life.

The example below is from the Summit Method worksheet:

Financials	Current	Year 1 Goal	Year 2 Goal	Year 3 Goal	Year 4 Goal	Year 5 Goal
Savings						
Committed Minimum Bank Account Balance	$2,000.00	$2,000.00	$2,000.00	$2,000.00	$2,000.00	$2,000.00
Average Monthly Savings Allocation	$1,500.00	$1,500.00	$2,000.00	$2,000.00	$2,500.00	$2,500.00
Current Total Cash Savings	$10,000.00	$28,000.00	$52,000.00	$76,000.00	$106,000.00	$136,000.00

Investments

 Investing in yourself with a solid, steady approach to growing your portfolio, your net worth, and assets over time is the best way to your *Financial Freedom*.

The next large chunk of cell input in the worksheet is for *Investments*. You can see that there is a lot to fill out here. Some cells won't apply to everyone because investments are a decision you make based on your unique situation and opinions.

As you fill in the standard investment strategies, it will automatically sum up your total investment gain that year. There are also some blank spots for adding investments if it is not already included, and you should delete any numbers that aren't applicable.

When you want to project that year's investment over 5 years, you will see that the worksheet is already programmed to calculate over time based on the average gain of that particular investment type. Feel free to adjust the percentage gain for your situation within the equation in the cells.

The goal is to take Year 1 of investments and effectively project what it could become over the next 5 years. One of the major reasons you invest is to ultimately amass enough wealth so you can retire, give back, be financially free to pursue your passions, or provide a legacy to pass down to your children.

The example below is from the Summit Method worksheet:

Financials						
	Current	Year 1 Goal	Year 2 Goal	Year 3 Goal	Year 4 Goal	Year 5 Goal
Investments						
401k	$200,000.00	$212,000.00	$224,720.00	$238,203.20	$252,495.39	$267,645.12
Retirement Brokerage Accounts (Total) Roth IRA, Traditional IRA	$56,000.00	$59,360.00	$62,921.60	$66,696.90	$70,698.71	$74,940.63
Other Retirement Accounts (Total) (Replace this cell with yours)	$100,000.00	$106,000.00	$112,360.00	$119,101.60	$126,247.70	$133,822.56
Liquid Brokerage Accounts (Total) Stock purchases, bonds, etc	$100,000.00	$106,000.00	$112,360.00	$119,101.60	$126,247.70	$133,822.56
Other Investments (Replace this cell with yours)	$0.00	$0.00	$0.00	$0.00	$0.00	$0.00
Other Investments (Replace this cell with yours)	$0.00	$0.00	$0.00	$0.00	$0.00	$0.00
Total Opportunity Cash in Investments	$456,000.00	$483,360.00	$512,361.60	$543,103.30	$575,689.49	$610,230.86

Retirement

When it comes to retirement, investments are going to be absolutely critical. While you will be getting money in social security depending on how long you worked, you will need to have other things set up to continue to support yourself during retirement. This financial planning exercise will help you see where you are today on your track toward retirement. There are some general rules of thumb for the retirement amounts you should have when you retire, but everyone's situation is different. The important part is that you are taking the time to focus on a plan, no matter your age!

General retirement rules of thumb when planning include, but are not limited to, the age-based investing schedule. Examples of age-based investing include:

- By the age of 30, have 1 year's yearly income invested in retirement.

- By the age of 40, have 2 times your yearly income invested in retirement.

- By the age of 50, have 4 times your yearly income invested in retirement.

- By the age of 60 have 8 times your yearly income invested in retirement.

For example: At the age of 60, let's say you make $100,000, this rule would require $800,000 invested into retirement accounts. If you are a corporate worker with a 401k with contribution matching and a long career, this would be fairly attainable.

This might not work for everyone though. Maybe your situation does not include a 401K, so what do you do?

You can open a pre-tax IRA or a post-tax Roth IRA to shovel money into the stock market and begin the compounding returns clock at any point in your career.

There are annuities, life insurance policies, and basic brokerage accounts, all designed to help you earn more than just the plain value of your money sitting in a bank account.

There are plenty of financial planners out there who will gladly work with you on one of the strategies above, and some of them are free for consultations and only charge once you start building a portfolio with them.

A partner of Conquer Your Summit provides a complete look at planning for retirement with an easy-to-use spreadsheet which can be found at www.ConquerYourSummit.com/retirementplanning.

If you have no idea where to start, a financial planner is probably the best resource for getting some kind of plan put together, but be warned, it's not the only way, and sometimes it's not the best way. Don't leave the planning to someone else, it's your life, learn how they plan and then apply it to your unique situation.

There is another camp of people who don't want to follow the above traditional work-life savings and investing. I would put these folks into the business or entrepreneurial bucket. In this camp, you are investing in your own business, managing your own brokerage portfolio, or investing directly in real estate or other assets as the owner. This generates passive income, or what is known as cash flow. Cash flow is the lifeblood of a business. If you're a business owner, your cash flow can maintain you in retirement.

As you become more financially aware and diversify your portfolio, it is recommended that you figure out ways to invest in passive income-generating assets. Some investors stick entirely to this strategy and never enter the traditional stock market. It works for them, but maybe it doesn't work for you. This is why learning about different options and your risk appetite is important. As you round out this section in the *Summit Method* worksheet, think about where you are and what you want to invest in. Now, make a plan to go achieve it!

If you feel lost about anything that has been discussed here, that is okay! That just means it's time to take a deep breath, put your *Mindset Change Muscle* to work, and start doing some research. The internet and AI platforms are a wealth of knowledge to get you started to find the right person to talk to. Reach out to our coaching if you need more help.

Filling Out Your Retirement Current State

For filling out the cells for *Retirement*, make sure you review what you put in for your *Current State*. You can then project your retirement growth over time based on the particular average increase that retirement strategy has per year. For example, the stock market has an average return of let's say 6%. You would take your current state retirement fund amount cell and then for each cell going forward in Years 1-5, the cells should be increasing by that 6%. Add in all retirement options you have going, project their growth, and then you can make sure it sums up the total. That total is what you will look at to see if you are roughly on target for retirement increases over the next 5 years with respect to your age-based invested fund number listed prior in this chapter.

Just like with the other sections, if the projections don't vibe with you, it's time to change your *Five-Year Plan* goals and projection cells to get to where you want to go. Then, start researching and working to climb that mountain and reach success.

The example below is from the Summit Method worksheet:

Financials						
	Current	Year 1 Goal	Year 2 Goal	Year 3 Goal	Year 4 Goal	Year 5 Goal
Retirement Where are you in retirement accounts right now?	$356,000.00	$377,360.00	$400,001.60	$424,001.70	$449,441.80	$476,408.31

Closing up

If you filled out the *Summit Method* worksheet correctly, the cells should add up to show you where you are today for income, expenses, debt, savings, investments, and retirement.

You might be jazzed right now because you just finished the most challenging content in the plan due to all the detailed work! You might also feel scared, sad, or confused depending on if it was challenging to complete. Remember the tools you packed in the backpack? You need to take those deep breaths and have a *Positive Growth Mindset* toward what you are accomplishing here. Remember: *a dream without a plan is just a wish.* Say goodbye to wishing. Put your life plan together and make your dreams a reality by perhaps:

- Implementing a method for getting out of debt.

- Earning more income to put into savings.

- Actually starting a savings plan.

- Growing your investments.

- Changing your job to change your money equation.

These are just some ideas!

Stressful? Yes. But I want you to think of this life change, whatever it may be, as great. Go forth and make changes in your life to better yourself.

At your next *Quarterly Check-In*, go into the worksheet and start altering those numbers to update your progress. Just think of what you can accomplish in 3 months if you set your mind to it!

 Next Steps Before Moving On

1. You don't need to fill out the *Summit Method* worksheet for finances yet, you will do that when you actually do your *Summit Event*. For now, go through the *4 Mountain of Success* Chapters 10-13 to learn how to do the planning techniques. Take any notes in your notebook from this chapter that you want to remember or use when you schedule your *Summit Event*.

2. If you are using the Conquer Your Summit workbook proceed to this same chapter number in the book to fill out the information.

Chapter 12

Create Your Career

This chapter is all about conquering your *Mountain of Career Success*. Let's get right into how to meet your *Career Success* goals for the next 5 years!

Complete Brainstorming Your Future

First, you must ensure your current state is filled out in the *Current Assessment* portion of the *Summit Method* worksheet. Then, you should have completed your Career Success Mind Map #6 on your career dreams in Chapter 8. Grab that from your notebook to review now. This next activity is a continuation of your Career Success Mind Map.

Record Your Journey: Career Success Mind Map Revamp

 Spend 5 minutes determining if there is anything you would like to add to your original Mind Map on *Career Success* based on further progress in the book. Think about companies, titles, positions, experiences, learning, trades, skills, complete career changes, etc. Think about where you might want to take your career in life and add to the mind map and themes you made.

Let's say someone is employed as a florist. Perhaps they dream of opening their own shop one day. Or they have goals of expanding their knowledge to a specialized skill in that trade. Possibly they are working toward obtaining a raise at the shop they are currently at.

There's so much one can do within any given profession to improve their situation! It's time for you to spend a moment to dive one step deeper into what *your* career could look like if you took the steps to improve your current state.

Make Your Career Sandwich

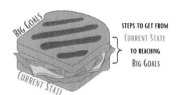

Go to your notebook where you did your career Mind Map and start picking out the things that speak to you the most—things you want to put into your plan over the next 5 years.

First, put a longer-term goal in the Year 5 cell that you want to strive for. With your current state already listed, you have a career planning sandwich in the making.

So far, you have two slices of bread: the beginning, and the goal. But the fun part of the sandwich is not the bread. (I know, bread is still pretty darn scrumptious! But we need actual nutrients...) Now, let's gather our ingredients!

Record Your Journey: Dive into Year 5!

Moving away from your *Summit Method* worksheet for a moment, in your notebook, I want you to write your desired end goal that you put in Year 5 and start a list underneath it. What do you believe the significant steps are to getting to that end goal? If you don't know, Google it, phone a friend, or find a mentor—now is the time for you to take life into your own hands and figure out the significant steps to getting to where you want to be!

Let's go back to the example of the florist. Let's say they have been working in their position for about 1 year. Let's say they aim to open their own shop, *Sassy Sunflowers: Creative Floral Designs to Spice Up Spaces*. Sounds pretty awesome, right?

Well, to make this dream a reality, they would need to start writing down the steps to get to that point. Maybe things like researching how to run a business, the costs of opening a shop, business loans, the market, how to make a business plan, and all the different things required to execute their business, such as supply chain, workforce, etc. They must dive into the business world quite a bit to start their own shop. This is an excellent exercise because maybe this person just loves being a florist and wants to expand to do more creative designs than their current shop allows them to do. They might realize through this exercise that they aren't that interested in all the business stuff, they just want to be able to grow in their skills and show off their creative side. That's great! That is precisely the point of doing this planning exercise.

Listing the Steps Reveals the Truth

The florist in this exercise has realized that they have a great idea and will seek other options that don't include starting something from scratch:

- They can network to find an entrepreneur who might want to invest in the florist's ideas with a partnership where they will run the business side of operations while the florist focuses on creative direction and roles that fit their interest.

- The florist could look for a business to buy that is already functioning, then come in and make some adjustments to their style.

- They could figure out how to work on convincing their current employer to try something new to augment the current business.

You will never know what you are truly capable of until you try.

Don't Let the Mind Limit You

People spend so much time in their heads, obsessing over possible negative outcomes until they end up convincing themselves something isn't possible.

Plot out your dreams in your career, walk through what steps are necessary to get to that point, and ask yourself if you align with that path. Repeat this exercise until you form a plan that makes you feel happy. Then, you can record it in your worksheet.

Take the bread ends of your *Career Success* sandwich and start putting in the micro growth improvements you can accomplish each year that will lead to getting to that end state in your career.

Set Reasonable Expectations

I want to clarify that 5 years is often not enough for all of someone's *Career Success* goals to be accomplished.

Let's say you decided your goal was to build a real estate investment company with 50 properties in the portfolio. You would notice that with all the steps involved to acquire that amount of properties, you might not be able to accomplish it in 5 years.

A sandwich can only hold so many ingredients! You have to put a reasonable amount of ingredients (steps) in your sandwich; otherwise, you won't even be able to take a bite out of it. Think bite-sized amounts throughout your multi-year progression, however many years that may be! But don't be afraid to take *some* big bites to push your growth! If you need to expand past the 5 years, it's okay to follow an expanded format and even think out to 10 years as needed.

Back to Your Career Success Worksheet...

When you fill in your *Summit Method* worksheet, write very clearly what the big end goal is for Year 5, the mini goals in between Years 1-4, and how you are going to accomplish them. Make sure you also fill in the basics: company, position, and skills you have or are growing in for each year.

Write in if you are looking to change companies or even change industries. It is okay to chart a course for a career you are not exactly sure how to enter. This is where mentorship comes into play.

Communication is a powerful tool. Let's say you want to be promoted at your job and it's part of your *Five-Year-Plan*. You can show your boss your *Five-Year Plan,* or select parts of it and ask them if they think it is reasonable based on how fast people get promoted at that particular workplace. If they are a good manager, they will help you look to see if it's realistic and give you pointers on the growth required to reach your goals. Because you have communicated with them, they will likely have you in mind when they need to promote people or when opportunities come up in your department.

Below is an example from the Summit Method worksheet for the first few years:

Career Five-Year-Plan	Year/ Age	Year 1 Goal	Year/ Age	Year 2 Goal	Year/ Age	Year 3 Goal
Where do you want to work? **What do you want to do?** **How do you want to make money?**	2023 33	**Person 1** **Company Name:** Company X **Title:** Title Y **New Skills:** Skill 1, Skill 2, Skill 3 **Other Goals:** Goal, Goal, Goal	2024 34	**Person 1** **Company Name:** Company X **Title:** Title Y **New Skills:** Skill 1, Skill 2, Skill 3 **Other Goals:** Goal, Goal, Goal	2025 35	**Person 1** **Company Name:** Company X **Title:** Title Y **New Skills:** Skill 1, Skill 2, Skill 3 **Other Goals:** Goal, Goal, Goal
	2023 32	**Person 2** **Company Name:** Company X **Title:** Title Y **New Skills:** Skill 1, Skill 2, Skill 3 **Other Goals:** Goal, Goal, Goal	2024 33	**Person 2** **Company Name:** Company X **Title:** Title Y **New Skills:** Skill 1, Skill 2, Skill 3 **Other Goals:** Goal, Goal, Goal	2025 34	**Person 2** **Company Name:** Company X **Title:** Title Y **New Skills:** Skill 1, Skill 2, Skill 3 **Other Goals:** Goal, Goal, Goal

Dealing with Fear and Worry

Maybe you are afraid to talk to your boss. Perhaps you are scared to find a mentor. Explore why you are afraid and why you have that worry. Ask yourself:

What is the worst that can happen from having this conversation?

No... Really... Take a moment and actually think through what YOU think the WORST that could happen would be.

Can you accept the worst-case scenario? If yes, then what are you waiting for? Go do it. Remember: being nervous, embarrassed, or scared is okay. If you have a *Positive Growth Mindset*, you know that every interaction is a learning experience, and you don't need to feel silly as you will be strong afterward.

Go into the conversation being open and honest. Say to your manager, "Hey, I am scared to have this conversation with you because I don't know what the outcome will be, and it makes me a little uneasy." You can set yourself free when you are transparent about your emotions, fear, and anxiety. You and your manager can then speak openly, and it becomes less embarrassing or scary. You both know it's a complicated conversation, and any good manager will help you through that.

Note: If your manager is not helpful or even difficult through this experience and you leave feeling like you got nothing out of it, it's time for you to think about where you are and your position in staying at that company. You should be given the respect you deserve.

Seek a Mentor in Your Field

You can find mentors simply by searching on LinkedIn for people in the same job as you or the job you want. Message them and ask them to connect because you want to pick their brain and you are looking for a mentor. You might need to contact a couple of people, but in the end, you will find someone to jump in and give you the real-life advice you need. Other options include doing an internet search on mastermind groups centered around the focus area you are looking for mentorship in. Investing in your education and bettering yourself will accelerate you to the end goal.

...Talk to someone who is actually living the life you want to live. Don't take advice from someone you wouldn't want to trade places with! Seek those who want to help you grow...

Some of you might be working towards climbing a ladder within a company, jumping to other companies, changing trades, starting businesses, and some in just getting to that initial career. If you are a student, your career is school right now. Use this plan to project your first job and what you are looking to do with it from there.

Everyone is different; write goals that fit your needs and get a mentor to help you get there faster.

Those who sit quietly expecting the world around them to know what they want and that everything will come together naturally will generally have slower progress. You must take your life by the horns and ride to the future.

 Next Steps Before Moving On

1. You don't need to fill out the *Summit Method* worksheet for your career yet, you will do that when you actually do your *Summit Event*. For now, go through the *4 Mountain of Success* Chapters 10-13 to learn how to do the planning techniques. Take any notes in your notebook from this chapter that you want to remember or use when you schedule your *Summit Event*.

2. If you are using the Conquer Your Summit workbook proceed to this same chapter number in the book to fill out the information.

Chapter 13

Connect with Your Community

The golden way is to be friends with the world and to regard the whole human family as one. – Mahatma Gandhi

This chapter is all about conquering your *Mountain of Community*. Let's get right into how to meet your *Community Impact* goals for the next 5 years!

Completing Your Brainstorming on Family and Friends

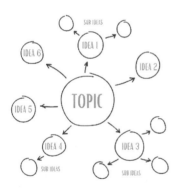

In previous chapters, you figured out the people in your family and friends group that mean the most to you so you could record the current state of your *Community Impact*. These are the people you want to have the most robust ongoing connections with and center goals around to ensure you are spending time with them. Review what you wrote prior to this in your notebook.

Record Your Journey: Community Mind Map 2.0

It's time to expand on your earlier thoughts. With your notebook, jot down answers to the following questions:

1. Do I want to make more friends?

2. Do I want to make different friends?

3. Do I wish I connected more with my family?

4. Are there relationships I would like to start nurturing?

5. Are there relationships I need to work on cutting out?

Do you have anyone in your current list you would like to grow your relationship with? Go back through your list and star people who need extra attention. Then, create a habit around making that relationship stronger.

I feel a goal coming on here. Perfect! You can now understand with whom or group of people you want to set a goal around. Maybe there are even some of those secondary list members you wish to bond with by setting a goal to become closer to them over the next year(s).

Start putting some of these family and friends interactions into SMART goal statements and add them to your *Five-Year Plan* timeline as you see fit. This category might not have things fully filled out in every single Year 1-5 but the important thing is to spend time thinking about it and charting out what makes sense. You might just want to keep a steady state of good intentions, progress, and maintain those relationships. This is perfect! Do what makes sense for you.

Your Yearly Community Impact Goals

For each year, answer the following statements in the cells of the *Summit Method* worksheet.

1. I want to keep strong relationships with the following people: *(list the names)*

2. I want to grow or create relationships with the following people: *(list the names, or for goals related to making new relationships, write New Person #1, New Person #2, and so on)*

3. Specific goals for a family member or friend: *(write any other goals you can think of here, example below)*

Examples in SMART goal format:

- *I want to help my mom with BLANK project by BLANK timeframe.*

- *I want to take my sister on a sister bonding trip by the end of this year.*

- *I want to plan and execute a family gathering this summer.*

- *I want to have BLANK friends come to visit me where I live this year.*

It can be anything you want to do with a specific family or friend member to try to hold yourself accountable to in your plan.

Focus on the Family That Is Close to Home

 Wherever you are in life, now is a great time to allow yourself some more profound thoughts on your most immediate family. Set a timer for 5 minutes and focus on the following exercise:

Take your notebook and write out some ideas on relationships of love—where you are, and where you want to be. If you are in a relationship, do you want to get married, have children, or have another child? Write down some thoughts here on timing and your reasons for yes or no.

If you have children, do you want to have different relationships with your children or raise them a certain way? Write it down.

If you are looking for love, do you want to start online dating, join meetups, or network with friends to find someone special in your life?

Start writing about your desires within this subject and remember you don't have to show it to anyone. You can rip it out and throw it away if you want to, but you owe it to yourself and your life to give yourself 5 minutes, at least, to think about these things, or longer. These thoughts can be challenging for some people, so make sure to go into it with a *Positive Growth Mindset.*

Even if nothing comes out of the exercise and into your plan, the fact that you gave yourself the time to think about it is incredible.

After 5-10 minutes, if there are any goals from this brainstorming that you want to graduate into your *Summit Method* worksheet, fill them in the Years 1-5 where they make sense. Remembering your age can help determine when to think about planning some of these items.

Goals for the External Societal Community

The external societal community is the last item to consider in your *Community Impakt* planning worksheet. This can be a wide range of things and will depend on what you do with your career and free time. These can be relationships you want to grow at work or how you interact with the public community. Grab your notebook and focus on the external community ideas that you might want to expand on from your first Mind Map in previous chapters, fill them into the worksheet over the years as you have been doing for the past several chapters.

Things to consider:

- Workplace coworker goals such as building up a team or gathering mentors.

- Community organizations such as churches, volunteer places, and community service.

- Any clubs or associations you are a part of or want to join such as sports teams, hobbies, networking groups etc.

You may find that you only know how to fill out the next couple of years. That's okay. You can always write the things you want to sustain long term into your Years 3-5 of the worksheet. The important thing is to spend the time trying to think that far in the future, just to make sure you identify things to work on now to get to the future state.

Coming up is how we will sustain all your goals through your *Two-Year Action Plan & Quarterly Goals*! Let's hop to it!

Community Five-Year-Plan	Year/Age	Year 1 Goal	Year/Age	Year 2 Goal	Year/Age	Year 3 Goal
	2023	Person 1	2024	Person 1	2025	Person 1
What goals do you have for your community?	33	**Family:** List Names and/or Goals **Friends:** List Names and/or Goals **External:** List Names and/or Goals	34	**Family:** List Names and/or Goals **Friends:** List Names and/or Goals **External:** List Names and/or Goals	35	**Family:** List Names and/or Goals **Friends:** List Names and/or Goals **External:** List Names and/or Goals
KEEP strong relationships with NAME?		**Legacy:** List Goals		**Legacy:** List Goals		**Legacy:** List Goals
GROW or create relationships with NAME?	2023	Person 2	2024	Person 2	2025	Person 2
Goals?	32	**Family:** List Names and/or Goals **Friends:** List Names and/or Goals **External:** List Names and/or Goals	33	**Family:** List Names and/or Goals **Friends:** List Names and/or Goals **External:** List Names and/or Goals	34	**Family:** List Names and/or Goals **Friends:** List Names and/or Goals **External:** List Names and/or Goals
		Legacy: List Goals		**Legacy:** List Goals		**Legacy:** List Goals

Next Steps Before Moving On

1. Chapters 10-13 taught you how to do the planning techniques. After you learn the *Two-Year Action Plan* and *Quarterly Goals* in the upcoming chapters you will be ready to have your very own *Summit Event*.

2. If you are using the Conquer Your Summit workbook proceed to this same chapter number in the book to fill out the information.

Chapter 14

Two-Year Details & Quarterly Goals

Now that you have completed the *Five-Year Plan* for your *4 Mountains of Success*, the *Two-Year Action Plan* and *Quarterly Goals* are next. Put your thinking cap on, and let's dive in!

How to Fill in Your Two-Year Action Plan

TWO-YEAR ACTION PLAN

You will see in the *Summit Method* worksheet that there are 2 full years listed by month. Depending on when you are doing your first *Summit Event*, you will start in the month you are currently in, finish up that year, and then fill out the following year for all *4 of your Mountains of Success: Personal Growth, Financial Freedom, Career Success, and Community Impact.* The goal is to focus on your execution while remembering to think across all *4 Mountains of Success*—this is the *Summit Method* way!

Reference your *Five-Year Plan* to pick out 1 or 2 things a month that will be your focus per *Mountain of Success*. Don't pick too many; choosing one is a great way to truly focus on success. As you fill this out, you may realize you have too many goals in your *Five-Year Plan* to be realistic. This is an iterative process, so you need to go through this to discover if things in your *Five-Year Plan* still make sense timing-wise. Do this for each success area and see where you get on your first pass. Then go through it for a second time to adjust until you believe you have a *Two-Year Action Plan* that is attainable and also aligns with your five-year projections.

When you complete this exercise, it will later be something you can reference for your *Quarterly Check-Ins*. During check-ins, ask yourself the following questions:

> *Am I completing things on time according to how long I thought it would take?*

> *Do I need to change my plans or goals based on new realities I might find?*

Don't get too hung up on the *Two-Year Action Plan*, just make bite-sized progress points. Its purpose is to enforce the *Five-Year Plan* and help you double-check if it makes reasonable sense to execute.

Example of the Two-Year Action Plan from the Summit Method worksheet:

	Year 1					
	January (Quarterly Check-in)	February	March	April (Quarterly Check-in)	May	June
	Goal	Goal	Goal	Goal	Goal	Goal
	Goal	Goal	Goal	Goal	Goal	Goal
Financials	Goal	Goal	Goal	Goal	Goal	Goal
	Goal	Goal	Goal	Goal	Goal	Goal
	Goal	Goal	Goal	Goal	Goal	Goal
Career	Goal	Goal	Goal	Goal	Goal	Goal
	Goal	Goal	Goal	Goal	Goal	Goal
Personal Growth	Goal	Goal	Goal	Goal	Goal	Goal
	Goal	Goal	Goal	Goal	Goal	Goal
	Goal	Goal	Goal	Goal	Goal	Goal
Community	Goal	Goal	Goal	Goal	Goal	Goal
	Goal	Goal	Goal	Goal	Goal	Goal
	Goal	Goal	Goal	Goal	Goal	Goal
Other	Goal	Goal	Goal	Goal	Goal	Goal
	Year 1					
	July (Quarterly Check-in)	August	September	October (Quarterly Check-in)	November	December
	Goal	Goal	Goal	Goal	Goal	Goal
	Goal	Goal	Goal	Goal	Goal	Goal
Financial	Goal	Goal	Goal	Goal	Goal	Goal
	Goal	Goal	Goal	Goal	Goal	Goal
	Goal	Goal	Goal	Goal	Goal	Goal

Your Quarterly Goals

QUARTERLY GOALS

Now that you have been limited to only a few goals per month in your *Two-Year Action Plan*, you need your 3 to 5 SMART goals for your current year. To do this, reference your *Five-Year Plan* and *Two-Year Action Plan* to determine the most important things to you or themes for your year. You get to use your heart and soul on this one and pick the items that need the most attention or you want to get done the most!

Review your *Five-Year Plan*. In your notebook, write down the supercritical things from any of your content in the *Personal Growth, Financial Freedom, Career Success, and Community Impact* sections. Do the same with the *Two-Year Action Plan* to make sure some of those vital things you just pulled out of your *Five-Year Plan* made the cut when you filled out the *Two-Year Action Plan*. If for some reason they didn't, make sure you update your *Two Year Action Plan* to have the most important things planned out. Take the top 3 to 5 and transfer them into SMART goals. *Reminder: SMART means Specific, Measurable, Attainable, Relevant, and Timebound.*

You want your year goals to be written very clearly. While they are goals for the year, you must focus on the *Timebound* aspect of the SMART goal. Assign each of these goals to be assessed at specific *Quarterly Check-In* dates during that year so you can track your progress at a reasonable time. Then, make sure you have a 3-month plan to execute that goal before its *Quarterly Check-In* due date. This is not a New Year's Resolution—you don't have all year to complete those goals and put them off! Keep your goal setting 3 months out and get those goals accomplished! *Quarterly Check-Ins* keep life planning fresh.

Once you have these *Quarterly Check-Ins* written and decided, you must create a step-by-step plan on how you will actually accomplish them. You should target 1 to 5 steps to get there and then plot those steps into the column for your 5-step plan in the *Quarterly Check-In* tab of the *Summit Method* worksheet. It's okay if you don't have a full 5 steps; the point is to think of an easy bite-sized plan without making it a 20-item list. That way you know exactly what you are supposed to be doing to actually complete your goal on time. Here is an example of a goal with the steps to accomplish it laid out in the worksheet:

Example of Quarterly Goals from the Summit Method worksheet:

Goal #	Quarterly Goals				
	Person 1				
	Title (1-2 word easy description or theme of the goal that you will remember)	SMART Objective	Plan What is your 5 step plan to get there?	Mountain of Success (Personal Growth, Financial, Career, or Community)	Deadline Which quarter check-in will it be done by?
1	Lose Weight	Lose 25 pounds by going to the gym and eating healthy by the end of the first Quarter on April 1.	1. Sign up for the gym 2. Sign up for classes 3. Go to classes 3 days a week 4. Throw away all junk food and purchase a book for healthy eating 5. Practice eating what the book teaches		Q1 April
2					
3					
4					
5					
6					

You have made it through the training part of your *Summit Event*! I'm so excited for you! When you complete your first *Summit Event*, you should feel proud of yourself and excited for life. Please reach out to me and let me know how the event went, I would love to hear about it and any feedback you have. To do that you can go to the Contact Us page of www.ConquerYourSummit.com/contact You will have accomplished something that most people do not bother to spend the time putting any focus into. Congratulations!

Beyond checking in with your *Summit Event* documents, there are some habit changes and daily practices that you must add to your life for the best results using the *Summit Method*—let's go over that next!

 Next Steps Before Moving On

1. Take any notes in your notebook from this chapter that you want to remember or use when you do your *Summit Event*.

2. Schedule your *Summit Event*! and actually do it!

Part Four Summary

In Part Four, you learned how to master creating goals for yourself projected out in a five-year time block for each of your *Mountains of Success*. You did this by creating:

1. **Five-Year Plan**

2. **Two-Year Action Plan**

3. **Quarterly Check-Ins**

Part Five is where you learn tools and techniques to be successful long-term in all of your climbs in life—and here you'll find an action plan that sticks! This is how you get to live your best life!

THE VIEW OF YOUR MOUNTAINS OF SUCCESS

Part Five

Conquer Your Summits Again and Again

When you climb a mountain, there will always be more mountains you will want to climb afterward. It's an exhilarating feeling when you get to the top! The world is full of beautiful places to explore and destinations that inspire your soul. After you have completed your first *Summit Event* and are working towards your check-ins with diligent execution, you have genuinely climbed to the peak!!!

Your skills and experience in mountaineering to your success lead you to be able to conquer your summits again and again. You gained mental tools and had the time and space to reflect, record your current state, and plan your climbs in life. You learned 3 new planning tools to pack into your backpack in doing this.

You have everything you need to succeed on the *Five-Year Plan*. But wait! There's more! In the next chapter, you will learn about motivation, habits, and daily execution tactics to change your life and keep your journey energized in the long term.

Mental Tools

Your Deepest Why

A Positive Growth Mindset

Mind-Body-Spirit Exercise

Planning Tools

Five-Year Plan

Two-Year Action Plan

Quarterly SMART Goals

Chapter 15

Motivation

You gain strength, courage, and confidence by every experience in which you really stop to look fear in the face. You are able to say to yourself 'I lived through this horror. I can take the next thing that comes along.' – Elenor Roosevelt

Life is daunting at times, with or without a plan. You, my friend, possess an incredible thing that will continue to catapult you into success. You have a plan! I have great faith in your ability to move forward and accomplish extraordinary things now that you are focused on following your map on this hike up to the mountain peak to accomplish your dreams.

Luckily for you, you have made new friends and connections along the way so you can be as successful as possible moving forward. These will be your accountability partners. You each decided to support each other in packing and prepping for the rest of the hike and will stick together for the big climb to the mountain peak. In this chapter, you will learn techniques about motivation to fuel your journey as you work towards your goals in life!

Healing the Mind Along Your Journey

To help with our motivation, we need to be more in touch with healing our minds.

Demotivation is natural, but it can be all-consuming. It is triggered by the brain's spiraling mess when we don't know what to do. This can lead to not wanting to do anything and being unable to progress.

While the next 3 items are bonus mind activities, don't forget about the *Mind-Body-Spirit exercise*, which you can do at any moment in time to force yourself to reflect within and center yourself to move forward. This alone can help catapult you right out of a mood and in the right direction.

Meditation

Some of you may already know the power of meditation, but others may not have learned how to unlock its greatness. For those of you rolling your eyes and thinking, *"Okay, let's move past this because I'm not going to meditate,"* I urge you to hear me out for a moment. Meditation is just a time of silence and reflection. For what you are doing here today, I want you to simply focus on clearing your mind.

You are constantly in the hustle and bustle of work, kids, family, friends, and commitments. Life is always throwing wrenches, so give yourself the space to disconnect. It's important to breathe and find a moment to clear your mind. Give yourself time to be truly in your mind and away from the world.

If you are alone right now, I want you to try something:

1. Close your eyes.

2. Get out of your head, and take a slow, deep breath.

3. Allow yourself to let go of the day and whatever is going on in your head. As you exhale, focus on the feeling of being alive.

4. As you try to clear your mind, thoughts may come into your mind, and that's okay. Simply observe those thoughts and focus on pushing them out for now, you can come back to them later.

5. Be okay with the silence, and don't force a thought if nothing is there. Enjoy that peace as the mind quiets down and your body melts into relaxation.

Think of this practice as a reset. This is you giving yourself the silence you need for you to have your own thoughts and not be affected by anyone around you. This is *your* time. All you need is one minute if you are in a rush. If you have the time, allow yourself to dive deeper into this space. Everyone's meditation is different, and you will learn to embrace whatever you need. The goal is just to introduce enough silence for the mind to reset.

As you sink into your meditative state, you will find the inner voice, your connection with the subconscious mind—your higher intelligence.

If you ever have trouble with motivation, practice coming to this state and pondering gently what kind of help you need. When you are in this meditative state, you will be surprised at what the subconscious mind will bring forward.

Put the book down and try this right now. If you aren't alone and don't feel comfortable, go find a place to do it. Taking this moment will go a long way.

Leaving Behind What No Longer Serves You

Would you keep a heavy backpack on your back full of life's heavy burdens forever without rest? Would you go to sleep with it? Work out with it? Probably not. So why are you carrying stuff around in your mind that no longer serves you?

The mind is a crazy place. There are so many things you can do to better your mind, but one thing to work on is freeing yourself from that which no longer serves you. The backpack was essential to you during the day as you run back and forth between the things you need to get done. But, when you go to sleep or decide you are ready to be freed from the weight, you need to learn to take it off.

Do not let people get in your head, and do not let the stresses of life consume you. You must find time daily to let go and be at peace with life. This practice is your springboard into greatness. Set the intention to free yourself of worry and maintain the open-mindedness required for future success in defining and accomplishing your goals.

Sometimes it is helpful to be proactive about recognizing things that do not serve you. Take a moment to think if there is anything in your life right now that is causing you stress or worry. Is anything bogging you down and creating weight on your soul? Things that can be in this bucket are:

- A lack of confidence

- Stubbornness

- Bad habits (drinking, unhealthy lifestyle, smoking, etc.)

- Thinking negative thoughts

- Having people around you that bring you down

- Procrastination

I want you to address anything in your life that does not serve you by creating a multi-step plan to tackle it head-on. Start by sharing the situation with someone else and get feedback from them. Visualize what your life would look like without these items and determine what the gap is between your current state and your ideal state with this issue.

Make a commitment in your notebook to carry the energy of the lifestyle you wish to have. When you feel lost and need motivation, read and review this page out loud.

Make Sure You Have an Accountability Partner

The best motivation tactic is having someone there for you when you need them most. They don't have to be someone who went through every step of the *Summit Method*, but you need to explain what you need them to do as your buddy in this next leg of the journey.

Share your *Quarterly Goals* and any parts of the life plans you created that you feel comfortable sharing. Now that they are aware, you will feel like you owe it to yourself and to your accountability partner to keep going. Your accountability partner is going to want to see you succeed. Call them up when times get dark and you lack motivation. They know their job is to lift you up. When you are tired on the trail, you have someone to sit next to you and open a snack to give you some energy to keep going. They will catch you when you fall and be there with all the tools you need to get you back on the life execution trail up to the top of the mountain. If you succeed, tell your buddy to join you and do their own *Summit Event*!

Discipline

One remaining item that you must make sure you are ready to pack in your bag is the art of discipline. Discipline is the fighting power we all have within us to get up each day and be ready to conquer.

You might even want to replace the word "discipline" with "clarity" because that's essentially what it is. Discipline is about making choices: you prioritize one thing over the other. To have the best year of your life, you need to be ready to have the clarity to put in the correct hard work, do the planning, execute, and check in...

rinse and repeat! This is having discipline which creates clarity on what you are focusing on.

Great things come from hard work and perseverance. No Excuses. – Kobe Bryant

On to the Next Mountain

Now that you have some essential tools for sparking your motivation, I want you to incorporate these practices into your habits. Make a solid effort to pull out these tactics whenever you feel resistance getting in the way of executing your goals. Remember your deepest *why* and stay focused.

You are now ready to walk fearlessly into the next leg of your hike. You are strong and can take down any barrier that comes your way. The mind is the sharp, swift knife you will use to cut through anything obstructing in your path. You can do it!

Moving forward from here means continuing the process. You have created the plans, are doing the mindset work, and can hit the *go* button. No map fully executes itself, though.

You must check in with the plan and ensure you are always on course!

 Next Steps Before Moving On

1. Practice completing a meditation session to clear the mind.

2. Determine what does not serve you in your immediate life bubble and work towards removing it from your mind.

3. Decide who your accountability partner will be and ask them to commit to helping you along the way.

4. Schedule and execute your first *Summit Event*. (If you didn't already!)

Chapter 16

Checking In

While climbing your life plan mountain, there will be rough terrain, distractions, snow, ice, wind, and cold. The environment can be unforgiving, but you are not afraid or worried because you have the best guide and gear for the job.

Making a written plan is not enough for you to truly accomplish all of your dreams and goals in life. You must be ready to key in on the next element: **Execution**.

Here, you will put all your plans into action, live your life, and deal with the stresses and barriers as they arise, but be focused on your end targets. When you do this, you are ready to climb the summits of your life!

What Comes After the First Summit Event?

My first *Summit Event* as you know, was held in an RV by the ocean and the best part about it was that it didn't just happen once. I got to continue having these adventures in various ways over the years to focus on my life plan execution.

Good planning involves implementation and checking in with the data as you go through life. Everyone has twists and turns along the way, so you have to be ready to adjust the decisions you make in your plan as you go.

Those who only look at their lives, goals, and plans once a year for a New Year's Resolution will not be successful. Life requires regular check-ins to get to the peak of your success. On this journey, you must:

- refuel

- take your time

- make calculated rest stops

- regularly review the map and compass (aka your plans)

- make sure your backpack and supplies are secured and ready to go at all times (to keep your motivation going)

...Don't forget your hiking team! Maybe you did the whole Summit Event with a partner. You may have an accountability partner you need to check in with as you go even if you did the Summit Event by yourself. The two of you need to take steps together as you climb, lending a helping hand as needed...

How Do You Accomplish This?

After your first *Summit Event*, start doing *Quarterly Check-Ins*. Focus on filling in your current progress and adjusting as needed. It's more of a review but with the mindset that you must be fully open to life changes that might reset some of your goals. That is why you need to actually plan out a time to do these check-ins and put focus into it. You must ensure you are on track to meet your targets and that your current goals are still what you want in life.

Get into a regular cadence for check-ins at the beginning of each quarter: approximately January 1st, April 1st, July 1st, and October 1st. It doesn't need to be right on the dot. You should set a calendar invite to be recurring for those dates every year in your life so you are reminded of them. This way, when you see this event coming, you can schedule your *Summit Event* on a weekend or day that works for your schedule and is roughly close to that ideal start-of-the-quarter date.

Life doesn't always work out perfectly, though. Sometimes I don't get to my January *Summit Event* until mid-January or early December. As long as you try to fit it in a 2-week range of the scheduled date, you will see progress.

Depending on what month of the year you are reading this book and planning to start your *Summit Event,* you will need to figure out which quarter start date is closest to you. If you are starting in November for example, you can claim that as the October 1st *Summit Event,* then be ready to jump in again for January 1st to start your regular 3-month cadence.

Your first *Summit Event* is intended to be a full day, take the course of several days, or be a full-on vacation. Whatever you do, make it a fun retreat. It is always healthy to get out of your everyday activities and make sure you spend enough time thinking about life without distractions. It's also a celebration, an acknowledgment of the fact that you are re-committing to self-love and taking responsibility for your life and your success.

...Don't let the concept of figuring out the perfect retreat be a deterrent to sitting down for your check-in. Maybe it's not a full retreat. Perhaps it's just a sit-down for half a day, pulling out the plan and making sure it still aligns. You need to do what is best for you and your life requirements, but you can't miss your check-ins at a bare minimum...

How to Do a Quarterly Check-In

What do these check-ins look like, and what do you need to do? Well, they can range from a full-blown retreat-type *Summit Event* all the way down to a quick half-day check-in. It will depend on your needs, how familiar you are with the *Summit Method* process, and what you want to accomplish.

I do not generally go to an entire vacation-like retreat every 3 months. However, that does sound amazing if you can swing it! I always try to schedule a retreat or vacation around my *Summit Event* once per year to connect with my partner and have fun along the way. Every 3 months, though, I schedule an entire Saturday and Sunday with my partner for our 3-month check-ins. Often this is at home, and we create a separate space to review our plans. We brainstorm new topics and set dedicated time for the analysis we need to do for the next 3 months. Selecting which of our *Quarterly Check-Ins* converts into a retreat outside of the home depends on our life schedule.

Whenever and wherever you have your quarterly *Summit Event*, the steps to accomplish it are easy:

1. Open your *Five-Year Plan*, *Two-Year Action Plan*, and *Quarterly Goals* to review if you are on track or need to make any changes.

2. Record the results from the last 3 months.

3. Make any changes to your plan going forward that are required.

4. Mark anything you finished or accomplished in the *Accomplishments* tab. This will be your running list of things you are proud of and have achieved.

An example of Check-Ins is shown below from the Summit Method worksheet:

Quarter				
Goal #	**Quarterly Check-Ins**			
	Quarter 1 April Summit Event	**Quarter 2** July Summit Event	**Quarter 3** October Summit Event	**Quarter 4** January Summit Event
1	**Complete?** When did you complete it? What was the result? **In Progress?** What steps are remaining? What is the new deadline date? **Cancelled?** Why? What happened?	**Complete?** When did you complete it? What was the result? **In Progress?** What steps are remaining? What is the new deadline date? **Cancelled?** Why? What happened?	**Complete?** When did you complete it? What was the result? **In Progress?** What steps are remaining? What is the new deadline date? **Cancelled?** Why? What happened?	**Complete?** When did you complete it? What was the result? **In Progress?** What steps are remaining? What is the new deadline date? **Cancelled?** Why? What happened?
2				
3				

TOP OF THE MOUNTAIN TIP

...Never forget to celebrate your accomplishments! It's important to give yourself credit and acknowledge the wins in your life. Be grateful and spend the time to soak in your progress...

What did you accomplish?	When?

+ ≡ -Year Plan - Career ▾   Five-Year Plan - Community ▾   Two-Year Action Plan ▾   Quarterly Goals ▾   Accomplishments ▾

Here are some handy things to ask yourself or think through at a *Quarterly Check-In*

- **Financial**: Record where you are (numbers-wise or description). Are you close to completion? What percentage are you at? (Record any completions in the accomplishment tab)

- **Quarterly Goals:**

  ○ Have you started your micro-step plan to get to that goal?

- ○ Why didn't you focus on that item in the past 3 months? (as applicable)

- ○ Is there something you would like to fix in life so you can focus on that item?

- ○ Is that item no longer essential to you? Why?

- ○ Do you need to remove it from your life plan because you have changed courses?

When you are done going through and recording your data on your current state for *Quarterly Check-Ins*:

- Open the *Your Deepest Why* tab on your *Summit Method* worksheet.

- Review your deepest *why* or your life purpose statement(s) to ensure it is still where you want to align yourself.

Remembering to be aligned with your life purpose statement will help you to make edits to your plans based on what truly matters to you.

Help! I am Not Reaching My Goals!

Let's say you still want to go for a particular goal, but you set yourself up for unrealistic deadlines in your progress. This is common in life planning, and you have the power to dive into what happened over the previous months during these check-ins. This will inform you of how you might need to adjust in the coming 3 months.

Look at your *Five-Year Plan*, and while filling out any updates to the current state, look at what you projected into your future. Is it reasonable? Do you want to add more because you accomplished so much with your focus?

The *Quarterly Check-Ins* are not only intended to make sure goals you set long ago actually happen; they are also for making sure you still want these particular goals to happen (since they are specific!). If you get rid of one goal, be sure to replace it with the new one you want to make come true! If you finish your goals, make sure you add more mini steps towards the next goal for the next check-in.

When you get into your *Two-Year Action Plan*, you will be able to look through the months and see if you were following along. This data measurement review is critical to understanding your trends as a planner and executor. The plan doesn't have current state cells to record where you are in the 3-month check-in because this form is meant to be a guiding light and show you how to finish and always be up to date. During your 3-month check-in, you should update the months to match what any of your new plans are based on the updates you might have made to your *Five-Year Plan*. It's your micro-step planner to reach your five-year success.

You should know precisely how you are doing for your *Quarterly Goals* since they were written as SMART goals with timelines in mind. *Did you make it? Yes, no, why not?* Reflect on yourself and think about the past 3 months. Create a new action plan for any goals that didn't get accomplished in that quarter. Start planning how to keep the rest of your year's goals on track over the remaining *Quarterly Check-Ins*. Think about how you want to do things differently from this point out. You can highlight goals in green if they were accomplished, and make sure to add them to your *Accomplishments* tab!

These Check-ins Have the Power to Change Your Life Course

The *Summit Event* is an event that my partner and I complete together. The whole process provides more value when we are together because it allows us to get out of our heads, bounce ideas off each other, and progress together. The conversations that form always enlighten our future and allow us to help each other in decision-making.

After our ocean-side RV *Summit Event*, time went by, and we did a shorter version at home for our check-ins for the remainder of the year. Each time we learned and evolved the process to become more effective for our needs and others. Over the years, we continued the back-and-forth cycle, updating and growing ourselves to succeed in the best ways possible.

I want to share with you an example of how a check-in can shift the course of your life decisions.

My Summit Event Pulled Me Through

I was utterly miserable working in my startup, where I was continually harassed and treated with a high amount of disrespect. I endured working there because I was a strong guiding leader to the engineering team. I sincerely felt I needed to be there to steer the team and enable them to be successful under such toxic leadership in the company. After spending many nights of tears and 3.5 years of pain, I finally had the courage to look in the mirror and make some new life decisions. I needed to review my plans and reflect on how I would make significant changes to stand up and fight for my mental health. I wanted to build a company the way I believed people should be treated, with respect.

I waffled about quitting the startup many times with one toxic person after another throughout my time there. When January came, I took my Summit Event retreat in the first week out into the wild. I took a whole week off, and my partner and I drove our Sprinter camper van through Death Valley. It was a downright incredible zen experience that I needed to disconnect from the pain of my job.

During this *Summit Event*, I realized, by looking through the data, that I couldn't afford to quit in January like I had wanted to. I knew that when I quit my job, I would take a 3-month sabbatical to reconnect with myself and heal from the mental trauma. I was going to need to be able to survive that period without pay, so it needed to be planned out. We discussed our *Personal Growth, Finances, Career, and Community* goals during the *Summit Event*. It was suddenly as clear as the brightest day that I needed to continue to work the painful job until at least March. Then I could afford to quit and start following my dreams. Before my January *Summit Event*, I was so blinded by the pains of my everyday life that I could not see the natural path I needed to take. Even though that path led to me continuing my pain for a bit longer, it was the right choice and set me up for future success.

These *Quarterly Check-in Summit Events* can be much more than just a written life plan review if you give them the time and energy. My partner and I find it a great time to have difficult conversations, pull up the brainstorming paper, and do detailed planning on a specific topic.

Your *Summit Event* Might Be the Missing Link

Your *Summit Event* is the time to research to see what big decisions in life need to be made and how to make them. Correct that course and get to where you are meant to go.

This forward energy carried me for the next 6 months until I finally left the aerospace industry to pursue different endeavors. I could look back proudly at what I had accomplished and be proud that I had the confidence to close that door with no intention of returning.

Life is meant to ebb and flow. I say *go with the flow*, even if that means it will set you on a completely different course and destination. It's the journey, not the destination, that makes you who you are.

 ## Next Steps Before Moving On

1. Schedule and plan your next *Summit Event Quarterly Check-In*. (Schedule your first *Summit Event* if you haven't done that either!)

2. Write down your micro-plan to reach your goals during the 3 months leading up to the check-in.

3. Decide which *Summit Event Quarterly Check-In* will be a retreat-like environment away from the home.

Chapter 17
Daily Advice

The new you is ready for change, to take action, and to see the results start flying in. One important thing to remember is that you can't expect your results to transform overnight without putting some effort into changing your habits or lifestyle first. Let's dive in.

If you say out loud a list of 10 things you need from the grocery store as you walk around the kitchen doing last-minute checks before running to the store, are you going to remember everything? You will most likely forget an item or two unless you write it down and check it off as you go along. The store is so massive, with distractions you will forget which items you had in your head while you go on a food scavenger hunt through the aisles. Even if you make a list, you are bound to forget items unless you diligently keep reviewing that paper. It is no different from your goals in life. You need to be reminded of them to make them happen, and it needs to be visual.

Making Your *Quarterly Goals* Visible Every Day

You have many things to keep track of and execute in your life plans. Let's start with the *Quarterly Goals*.

We know the concept of having yearly goals is outdated and that New Year's resolutions rarely hold for people. This is why we have the regular *Quarterly Check-Ins* in place with time-bound progression throughout the year so you can't just procrastinate or give up on your yearly goals.

For these *Quarterly Goals*, I want you to print them out or write them on a piece of paper. Then tape them to your bathroom mirror so you see them daily when you brush your teeth.

Other great spots include right next to your door as you exit your bedroom, your main house door, your nightstand, your wallet, or your phone (anything that you use daily). As you scan the list, tell yourself which micro step you will take that day to reach your goals.

As the days pass and you look at your goals daily, you will find yourself in 1 of 2 situations:

1. You are killing it by making the needed progress!

2. You are stagnating because you haven't put focus into it.

Camp #2 happens if you have not done anything towards those goals or followed the mini-steps you created. To solve this, you must have an emergency sit-down *Summit Event* with yourself and ask yourself *why*. Why are you not actually following the plan you laid out for yourself?

1. *Do you need to adjust the goals?...* Go fix them to align better with your passions.

2. *What is the root cause of your lack of progress?...* Identify if there are other parts of your life you need to fix to give yourself the space to actually do these mini steps.

3. *What are your barriers to progress?...* Write them down in your notebook so you can hold yourself accountable for cutting out those barriers.

This can be a very short 1-hour event. Just open your written plan and review your life purpose vision. *Are you still aligned?*

Once you figure out how to guide yourself back on track with solid motivation, keep going, and at the first of every month, ask yourself, are you making progress or not?

During your daily acknowledgment of your goals and mini plans (written on the wall somewhere easy to see), you must actually follow your detailed action plans to make progress. At the end of each week, write on your sheet on the wall with a pen the percentage of progress you think you made that week. That or a tally mark for each day you did one thing towards a goal. How many tally marks did you get in a week? That way, you keep seeing a visual indicator of how you are doing. You only have 3 months till your next check-in, so there is no time to waste or procrastinate.

Taking Your Notebook to the Next Level

 Another solid habit to develop is figuring out a way to look at your high-level goals, vision, and inspiration daily. Remember that notebook you used during this book? Don't throw it out. I want you to keep using it. If you feel like you want to upgrade to something more awesome and fun that you enjoy writing in, great! Go for it. I want you to keep a notebook or journal during your daily check-in to reach your goals. Before you roll your eyes or say, *"Nah, that's not for me,"* give it a chance.

Do you want to change your life or not? A notebook is a small ask when it comes to transforming your life.

In addition to putting up signs in your house, get into the habit of picking up your notebook daily. Create a few pages with this notebook that spell out your goals and detailed steps to accomplishing them. Here are 5 things to lay out in your notebook.

1. Write or tape a printout of your *Quarterly Goals* on the first page. Yes, you also need to paste it somewhere visual in your house.

2. On the second page, write or tape a printout of the weekly tasks required to reach those goals before their due date.

3. The third page is reserved for you to write or tape a printout of your vision or life purpose.

4. The fourth page can be where you write out your affirmations in a dedicated spot like you started to at the beginning of this book. Here you can build on them and add inspirational quotes or sentences to keep your energy flowing.

5. The fifth page (spread open as one giant page) should be the fun, colorful visualization of your vision. Paste pictures of your inspirations and anything that will help you get excited about your vision and goals when you see them. You might draw or paste a picture of a beach vacation

to inspire you to keep saving money for a vacation. You might draw or paste a picture of a fitness model to help you with your strength weightlifting goals. Other ideas include showing someone working in the career position you are looking for, attending the school you want to attend, or volunteering at organizations in your community. Make sure you remember your *4 Mountains of Success: Personal Growth, Financial Freedom, Career Success, and Community Impact,* and put things on this page to inspire your brain to get excited about life!

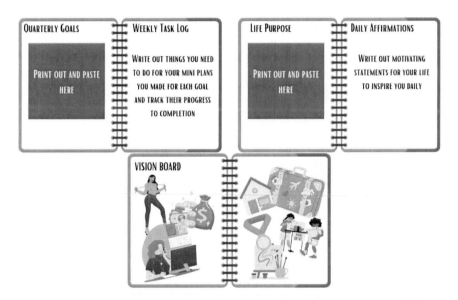

Your vision pages should align with the *Five-Year Plan* and *Two-Year Action Plan* you did but be an exciting visual aid to reaching that success. Visualization can be a powerful push to drive you to success. Make sure it's meaningful and sets your sights high.

After your vision pages, start writing freely to journal anything along the way or have a place for detailed planning as needed. Your notebook is a great place to track what steps you plan to make toward a goal and verify your progress the next day. You don't have to write a daily diary about what you did with your day, but writing down some items about your progress, thoughts, and needs along the way will help.

I have a notebook where I review my vision board and track short-term and long-term goals. I see things I need to focus on for that week and write them into my daily entry logs. It works very well, and it's data-driven.

Data Will Set You Free

Each day, you will see the data and make progress. I had a mini goal to write letters to my grandma, and I am reminded daily to make sure it happens once a month. I have now effectively started doing the letters more often, sometimes it doesn't happen as much as I like but the visual reminder gets me back on track. In the past, I always just forgot, and it never happened. Visuals will change your life and seeing the data will keep you on target.

Tracking all of your important habits will make it so your mind can't find excuses and illusions of progress. Data will set you free and speak the real truth about what is going on. Record the data, and review the real progress.

Keep It Simple

This doesn't have to be a long lengthy process. Just grabbing the notebook first thing—maybe next to the nightstand—and reviewing it will set the course of your day in the right direction. Some days will be busy, and perhaps you won't get to it, but if you try to do this daily, it will get you on the right track and put you above most people.

This practice will help you with things like:

- the reminder to eat healthy because you will see the setbacks tomorrow if you binge eat

- the kick you need to plan a family event or call your mom

- the inspiration to stop waiting and sign up for a training program you wanted to do today

Using your notebook daily will allow you to be quickly reminded of your goals and vision with ease.

 Next Steps Before Moving On

1. Paste your *Quarterly Goals* somewhere you will see them every day.

2. Build your goals, mini-plan, purpose statement, and vision board into your notebook.

3. Review your notebook each morning to set you on the right course.

Part Five Summary

With the completion of this last part of the journey, you have gathered the tools required to relieve the burden and anxiety around planning for life's dreams and goals! Those tools included:

1. Additional mental tools for motivation:

   - Meditation

   - Leaving behind what no longer serves you

   - Make sure you have an accountability partner

   - The art of discipline to find clarity

2. How to plan and execute a *Quarterly Check-In*

3. Daily execution habits to accelerate your progress

   - Posting goals & week plans in an easy plan to see every day

   - Upgrading your notebook to show your goals, life purpose statement, mini steps towards your quarterly progress, and a vision board to inspire you

Part Five set you up for long-term success to be able to tackle any mountain that comes your way. You can create action plans that stick so you see your progress flourish along the way. All you must do is get out there and keep the energy going!

Once you have conquered a summit, you will want to try your hand at others. You'll find that just the act of going for it is a thrill in itself.

What Now?

The air is crisp and cool. Oxygen is limited. The sun is twinkling upon the ice and snow at your feet. You see a collection of flags popping out of the snow up ahead in vibrant shapes and colors.

You can tell many others have been here before you and completed the task. Inspired by what you see, you are ready to take the last 50 feet with courage and excitement.

There are a couple of tough ice ledges and scrambling between you and the finish line, but you have your accountability partners there with you on the hike. Each of you helps the other set up ropes and survey the landscape for optimal climbing safety directions.

One by one, you scale up. As you throw your climbing pickaxe up to the high ledge and pull yourself up, you are amazed at the sight. There is a silence in the air like nothing you have ever experienced, and it is only broken by the cheers of your fellow hikers who just made it over the final ledge as well.

As a team, you stake down the victory flag you brought up with you to add to the sea of colorful flags. You are proud to be placing your victory flag among other strong mountaineers before you. You can see views of majestic mountains and glaciers below that appear to go on endlessly. You realize that the journey you have completed has set you up mentally, physically, emotionally, and spiritually to conquer any summit that comes your way.

You should take as much time as necessary at the peak to soak in the feeling of achievement. You deserve every minute of this incredible view overlooking the landscape for the rest of your life.

Look How Far You've Come!

Take a little time to reflect. Observe how far you have come on this journey and the new person you have become along the way:

You started this trek with nothing but the basic mental tools required to get through your journey.

You learned how to harness your *Mindset Change Muscle* at different points along your journey, which changed your life before you even started the hike.

At Base Camp, you gathered what your current state was from the trek's first leg and then completed the projection of your life going forward into your *Five-Year Plan* and *Two-Year Action Plan*.

You acclimated to the environment by analyzing your data, developing decision-making techniques, and exploring the motivation required to reach the final stretch.

While climbing to the top of the last *Mountain of Success*, you learned the final steps of how to accomplish *Quarterly Check-ins* with effective daily techniques to optimize your new lifestyle.

Now you have stepped into success with the *Summit Method*.

What Now?

 Within the time it took to read this book, you probably haven't completed your goals yet, but you will. You know the process to get there, and the techniques required for success.

Make the 30-day promise!

- Schedule and execute your first *Summit Event*

- Prepare your notebook

- Implement a daily tracking practice

Go to your calendar and schedule when you will complete your first *Summit Event* whether it's a retreat or something at home.

Make it happen! *What do you have to lose?*

If you are serious about implementing the content of this book and living your best life, visit www.ConquerYourSummit.com/coaching for help to get there!

Share Your Journey with Others

My life purpose is to help others and create a rippling effect to change the world. Through small actions, I hope I can make a difference in people's lives. I can only accomplish this with your help in spreading the word to those who could use some helpful advice in life planning.

If you enjoyed learning the *Summit Method*, I want you to go out and share what you have learned from this book and invite others to join you. Ask them to start their own journey to conquering their summits.

Happy Hiking, See you on the trail to your dreams!

—Aliki Samone

Acknowledgments

I would like to thank the following people for making this book possible:

Abel, for loving and supporting me through the journey to becoming an author even when times were tough.

My family for always being there to encourage me in my crazy ideas and pursuits.

Sandra Wissinger, my editor, for helping me turn this book into a reality and together getting my message across the way it was meant to be written.

Self-Publishing.com for guiding me from knowing nothing about writing a book to start my career as an Author and filling my life with purpose.

Books change lives.

Author Bio

Aliki is a dynamic entrepreneur fueled by a blend of science and creativity. As a multi-talented artist, she is a singer-songwriter, creative author, and paints abstract art usually in the form of murals. With a lifelong love for nature, she embraces adventure and finds serenity in the great outdoors.

After a decade in spacecraft design and program management, she left the industry to pursue a life of passion and build her own businesses. Drawing from this wisdom and her connection to nature, she developed the Summit Method to be a holistic approach to planning your life.

Her passion for exploration is evident as she travels in her camper van, seeking new hiking, kayaking, and climbing challenges. Aliki aspires to inspire others to pursue their passions, reaching for the stars with her life experience as a guide.

The bigger the mountain, the more diverse the journey, and the more exciting the challenge becomes! – *Aliki Samone*

Can You Help Me Out?

Thank You for Reading My Book!

I really appreciate all your feedback and I love hearing what you have to say.

I need your input to make the next version of this book and my future books better.

Please take two minutes now to leave a helpful review on Amazon letting me know what you thought of the book, This will help me get the book into the hands of more people and expand the ripple effect of change.

www.ConquerYourSummit.com/review

Thanks so much! – Aliki Samone

Made in United States
North Haven, CT
02 June 2024

53209080R00102